An introduction to supporting people with a learning disability

Series Editor: Lesley Barcham

Mandatory unit and Common Induction Standards titles

Communicating effectively with people with a learning disability
ISBN 978 0 85725 510 5

Personal development for learning disability workers ISBN 978 0 85725 609 6

Equality and inclusion for learning disability workers ISBN 978 0 85725 514 3

Duty of care for learning disability workers ISBN 978 0 85725 613 3

Principles of safeguarding and protection for learning disability workers
ISBN 978 0 85725 506 8

Person centred approaches when supporting people with a learning disability
ISBN 978 0 85725 625 6

The role of the learning disability worker ISBN 978 0 85725 637 9

Handling information for learning disability workers ISBN 978 0 85725 633 1

Titles supporting a unit from the level 2 health and social care qualifications

An introduction to supporting people with autistic spectrum conditions
ISBN 978 0 85725 710 7

An introduction to supporting people with a learning disability
ISBN 978 0 85725 709 3

An introduction to supporting people with a learning disability

Elaine Hardie and Liz Tilly

Supporting a unit from the level 2 health and
social care qualifications

Los Angeles | London | New Delhi
Singapore | Washington DC

all about people

Learning Matters
An imprint of SAGE Publications Ltd
1 Oliver's Yard
55 City Road
London EC1Y 1SP

SAGE Publications Inc.
2455 Teller Road
Thousand Oaks, California 91320

SAGE Publications India Pvt Ltd
B 1/I 1 Mohan Cooperative Industrial Area
Mathura Road
New Delhi 110 044

SAGE Publications Asia-Pacific Pte Ltd
3 Church Street
#10-04 Samsung Hub
Singapore 049483

Editor: Luke Block
Development editor: Helen Fairlie
Production controller: Chris Marke
Project management: Deer Park Productions
Marketing manager: Zoe Seaton
Cover design: Pentacor
Typeset by: Pantek Media, Maidstone, Kent
Printed by: Ashford Colour Press Ltd

BILD
Campion House
Green Street
Kidderminster
Worcestershire
DY10 1JL

© 2012 BILD

First published in 2012 jointly by Learning Matters
an imprint of Sage Publications Ltd and the British
Institute of Learning Disabilities.

Library of Congress Control Number: 2011945616

British Library Cataloguing in Publication Data

A catalogue record for this book is available from the
British Library

ISBN: 978 0 85725 709 3

MIX
Paper from
responsible sources
FSC
www.fsc.org
FSC® C011748

Contents

This book covers:

- The Level 2 health and social care unit LD 201 – Understand the context of supporting individuals with learning disabilities

---

Acknowledgements

Photographs from www.thepowerofpositiveimages.com, www.careimages.com and www.crocodilehouse.co.uk. Photos have also been reproduced from issues of *Apex* and from the BILD publication, *Crossing Boundaries*. Our thanks to James and Tina Cooper, Sophie, Janet, Lois, Peggy Fray, Frances, Our Way Self Advocacy and Choices Housing.

About the authors and the people who contributed to this book

Elaine Hardie

For 11 years Elaine worked in services for people with learning disabilities, during which she was committed to a multi-disciplinary approach to risk enablement and person centred planning. Elaine also worked for eight years as a training officer and then social services training manager.

Elaine worked for BILD for five years delivering training for staff across the health and social care sector as well as developing policies and procedures for a number of local and national organisations. She is a tutor, assessor and internal verifier for a range of qualifications. Elaine has had several books published by BILD including the *Induction Award Trainer Pack* and *A Brief Guide to the Mental Capacity Act*.

Liz Tilly

Liz is strongly committed to the full inclusion of people with learning disabilities in all aspects of life, and has had regular professional and social contact with people with learning disabilities for over 30 years.

Liz works as a freelance trainer and consultant and also set up and is a director of Building Bridges Training, a social enterprise of people with a learning disability which provides training. Liz founded and was chief executive of a voluntary organisation in the West Midlands which provides a wide range of services and opportunities for people with learning disabilities. Prior to this, her career was in special education.

She has learning disability qualifications including a B.Ed. and M.Med.Sci. as well as an M.A. in applied social research. Liz is currently doing a Ph.D. researching the needs of and support to people with mild learning disabilities who fall through the net of statutory provision.

Janet Jones

Since the deaths of both of her parents, Janet has lived in the family home with her brother. Janet is very capable within her personal and work life, and is still dependent on her links with day services and the friendships she has had for many years. During the course of her employment at New Ventures, Janet has grown in personal and professional confidence and she enjoys transferring her skills and knowledge when working in other environments. Janet has a natural way of supporting other people with learning disabilities who have complex needs; she shows empathy, gives the right level of support and is aware of confidentiality, respect and dignity.

Mike Pye

Mike has never accessed adult services since leaving school. At first, he was sceptical about starting work at New Ventures but now works two days a week. He hates to miss a day and takes his responsibilities seriously. Mike has grown in confidence and is excellent at mentoring new staff.

Mike also enjoys his free time, when he likes to go off for the day to visit different places on his own. This is usually by train and nowhere seems to be too far! Mike goes on foreign holidays several times a year with his step dad or cousins. Mike values the friendships he has made during his employment – people within New Ventures and those he comes across in day services, as well as those from his past.

James and Tina Cooper

James lives in his own bungalow in the West Midlands and leads a full life in the community and with his family. He receives 24 hour support from a day service, a local care provider and his family. James loves swimming, music, going out to eat, watching football and motor racing. His mother Tina was James' main carer when he lived at home, until three years ago. Tina and the rest of the family supported James to get his own home and arrange his support using a personal budget. Tina has supported other people with learning disabilities and their family carers to get a good life through self directed support. Tina is a director of Time 4 People, an organisation that provides training, consultancy, presentations and information on all aspects of personalisation. For more information go to www.time4people.org.uk

An introduction to supporting people with a learning disability

David, Patty, Rosie, Steven, Pat, Jo, Keith, Val and MacIntyre

Liz Tilly would like to thank the many people supported by MacIntyre who worked with her to provide their ideas and stories about what good support means to them. For more information about MacIntyre go to www.macintyrecharity.org.uk

Introduction

Who is this book for?

An Introduction to Supporting People with a Learning Disability is for you if you:

- want a comprehensive introduction to supporting people with a learning disability;

- work in an organisation that sometimes has customers with a learning disability, for example a bank, leisure centre or surgery, and you want to be able to provide them with a good service;

- work in health or social care with people with a learning disability and you want to have a better understanding of how to provide good support;

- are a manager in a service supporting people with a learning disability and you have training or supervisory responsibility for the development of your colleagues;

- are a direct payment or personal budget user and are planning learning opportunities for your personal assistant.

Links to qualifications

This book gives you all the information you need to complete the level 2 unit, *Understand the context of supporting individuals with learning disabilities* from the level 2 and 3 diplomas in health and social care as well as the level 2 and 3 learning disability certificates and award. You may use the learning from this book to:

- work towards a full qualification e.g. the level 2 or level 3 diplomas in health and social care, or a level 2 or 3 certificate or award;

- achieve accreditation for a single unit on understanding people with a learning disability.

Although anyone studying for the qualifications will find the book useful, it is particularly helpful for people who provide services to or who support people with a learning disability. The messages and stories used in this book are from people with a learning disability, family carers and people working with them.

Links to assessment

If you are studying for this unit and want to gain accreditation towards a qualification, first of all you will need to make sure that you are registered with an awarding organisation which offers the qualification. Then you will need to provide a portfolio of evidence for assessment. The person responsible for training within your organisation will advise you about registering with an awarding organisation and give you information about the type of evidence you will need to provide for assessment. You can also get additional information from BILD. For more information about qualifications and assessment, please go to the BILD website: www.bild.org.uk/qualifications

How this book is organised

Each chapter covers one learning outcome from the qualification unit *Understand the context of supporting individuals with learning disabilities.* The learning outcomes covered are clearly highlighted at the beginning of each chapter. Each chapter starts with a story from a person with learning disability or a family carer or a worker. This introduces the topic and is intended to help you think about the ideas from their point of view. Each chapter contains:

 Thinking points – to help you reflect on your practice;

Stories – examples of good support from people with learning disabilities and family carers;

 Activities – for you to use to help you to think about your work with people with learning disabilities;

Key points – a summary of the main messages in that chapter;

References and where to go for more information – useful references to help further study.

At the end of the book there is:

A glossary – explaining specialist language in plain English;

An index – to help you look up a particular topic easily.

Study skills

Studying for a qualification can be very rewarding. However, it can be daunting if you have not studied for a long time, or are wondering how to fit your studies into an already busy life. The BILD website contains lots of advice to help you to study successfully, including information about effective reading, taking notes, organising your time and using the internet for research. For further information, go to www.bild.org.uk/qualifications

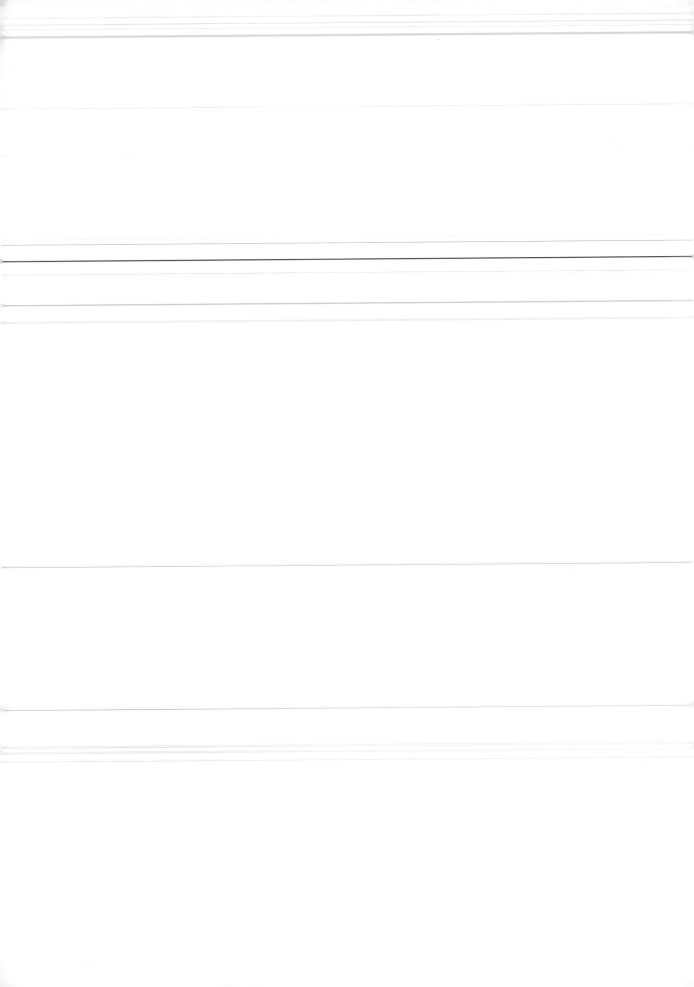

Chapter 1

Understanding the nature and characteristics of learning disability

Daniel loves action films, and going to the cinema. He never misses an episode of *EastEnders*, and enjoys watching Formula One racing and rugby on TV. He loves a pint in the local pub and to tease and have a joke with his friends. He hates waiting at bus stops, especially when it is raining. He lives with his mates Luke and Ray; they argue whose turn it is to wash up but otherwise they get on really well. In the daytime Daniel spends half the week volunteering at a local centre for older people and half the week at a day service for people with a learning disability. His dream is to go on holiday to Las Vegas and get a paid job. Daniel has a learning disability.

Emma, Daniel's key worker

Karen lives in north Lincolnshire in her own flat. She has had a part time job in a supermarket for the past 12 years; Mencap's specialist employment service helped her to get her job. Karen says, 'I particularly enjoy meeting customers and helping them out. My job is important to me, because it gives me money to do the things I am interested in.' Karen is involved in lots of community activities including a Mencap group, a self advocacy group and the local partnership board. She says, 'People don't always listen to what we (people with a learning disability) have to say, but more people are listening than ever before – the more people ... speak up, the better the chances of changing things for the better.'

You can read more of Karen's story at www.mencap.org.uk/all-about-learning-disability

James is in his late twenties, he has his own home and he leads a busy life. He enjoys looking smart and being out and about with friends and family. James loves his garden and he uses a remote camera to keep an eye on the wildlife. James doesn't use words to communicate but his family, friends and the people who support him know a lot about what he is saying by watching his body language and facial expressions. James has a number of medical and mobility needs. As James' family we know that he has a profound learning disability and he needs support in every part of his life, but our aim is for him to have a good life. His dad and I support him regularly in his own home and we often go out with him on local trips. I am the person who knows James best. I sometimes help to train the team of workers that support him; I speak up for James and make sure he gets the right support.

Tina Cooper, mother of James.

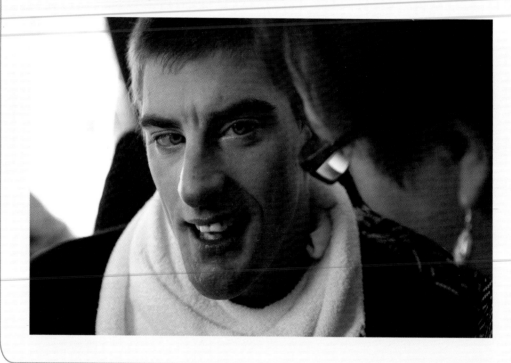

Introduction

The accounts above about Daniel, James and Karen show us that people with a learning disability are just like you and me; they have hopes and dreams, homes and jobs, family, favourite TV shows, football teams and music. They love to achieve and be appreciated, laugh and enjoy life. People with learning disabilities are equal citizens and have the same rights and responsibilities as all of us. In order to provide a good service to a person with a learning disability or to support them to achieve their rights, you need to know a bit more about what it means to have a learning disability.

This chapter will help you understand what is meant by the term 'learning disability' and it will explain some of the causes of learning disabilities. Significantly, it will help you to identify some of the barriers that people with a learning disability, and their family carers, see to them being accepted as equal citizens.

Learning outcomes

This chapter will help you to:

- understand what is meant by a 'learning disability';

- explain possible causes of learning disabilities;

- describe the medical and social models of disability;

- know about the approximate proportion of individuals with a learning disability for whom a cause is 'not known';

- understand the possible impact on a family of having a member with a learning disability.

This chapter covers:

Level 2 LD 201 – Understand the context of supporting individuals with learning disabilities: Learning Outcome 2

What is a 'learning disability'?

The term learning disability is a label; it is used as a convenience in discussions and planning, for example in health and social services. However, the reality is that everyone who carries that label also carries many other labels, for example sister, father, friend or colleague. A label only ever describes one aspect of a person. We are all much more than the labels that might be used to describe us. A person with a learning disability is always a person first.

Thinking point

What labels would other people use to describe you? Do any of these labels have positive or negative associations?

Definitions of learning disability and learning difficulties

Language is changing all the time. The words we use to describe a particular impairment or disability change as a result of listening to people with personal experience and as a result of changing values and attitudes in society. In addition, the same words can have different meanings in different countries. Although we share a common language with countries such as America and Australia the words we use to describe particular disabilities related to learning are different.

People can often find the term 'learning disability' confusing because there are several different explanations about what a learning disability is. Learning disability and learning difficulties are terms that are commonly used in the UK. These two terms are often interchangeable when used in the context of health and social care for adults. Some people with learning disabilities prefer the term learning difficulties.

People First, an advocacy organisation, says:

At People First (Self Advocacy), when we talk about people with learning difficulties, we mean 'people labelled as having a learning difficulty'. This is one of the labels that society puts on us to mark us out as not being able to understand things the same as other people... We believe that people labelled as having a learning difficulty are disabled by society. We choose the term 'learning difficulty' instead of 'learning disability' to get across the idea that our learning support needs change over time.

For more information on People First go to www.peoplefirstltd.com

There are several definitions of learning disability used in the UK. A commonly used one is from *Valuing People: a new strategy for learning disability for the 21st century*, the government White Paper for England about health and social care support for people with a learning disability (2001). It explains that a learning disability includes the presence of:

- a significantly reduced ability to understand new or complex information or to learn new skills;

- a reduced ability to cope independently;

- an impairment that started before adulthood, with a lasting effect on development.

This means that the person will find it harder to understand, learn and remember new things, and means that the person may have problems with a range of things such as communication, being aware of risks or managing everyday tasks.

> *Josie, a woman with Down's syndrome, explains how having a learning disability affects her:*
>
> You get stuck a lot. My sister helps me with sorting out my money.

In UK education services, the term 'learning difficulty' includes children and young people who have 'specific learning difficulties', for example dyslexia, but who do not have a significant general impairment of intelligence. The Special Educational Needs codes also use the terms 'moderate learning difficulty', 'severe learning difficulty' and 'profound multiple learning difficulty', which relate to general impairments in learning of different severity. These could be seen as interchangeable with the term 'learning disability' which is used in health and social care, and the groups of mild, moderate, severe and profound learning disabilities explained below. Further information about definitions can be found at www.improvinghealthandlives.org.uk, www.bild.org.uk and www.bris.ac.uk/cipold

Finally, when thinking about different definitions it is important to know that the UK is the only country that uses the term learning disability in the way described above. In other English speaking countries the term 'intellectual disability' is growing in usage. For the first time in the UK a report by Professor Jim Mansell, for the Department of Health, called *Raising Our Sights: services for adults with profound intellectual and multiple disabilities* (2010) used the term intellectual disability instead of learning disability. This could indicate that we are on the cusp of a change in the use of language in the UK. In the 1970s the term to describe people with a learning disability changed from people with mental sub normality to people with a mental handicap. And again in the 1990s the language changed from people with a mental handicap to people with a learning disability. Another change may now be about to occur – only time will tell.

In America the term 'learning disability' has a different meaning to that used in the UK. In the USA, learning disability is used to cover several specific learning disorders particularly in relation to reading, writing and maths, such as dyslexia, dyspraxia and dyscalculia. The terms 'intellectual disabilities' and 'mental retardation' are commonly used as labels to describe what we in the UK would understand as learning disabilities.

The term 'learning disability' is used to describe a very varied group of individuals. This includes people who have high levels of care needs such as James, in our introduction, to those who only need support in a few areas such as budgeting or accessing healthcare. Categorising people into groups on the basis of their disability is almost as bad as labelling them. In many ways it is for the convenience of those planning and delivering services, and it does not benefit the people being placed into a certain group. However, if you are to understand learning disability then you need to know that in the UK we have been categorising people in relation to the nature of their needs or level of disability for over 100 years. We currently use the terms profound, severe, moderate and mild to make a distinction between different levels of need. These categories are not rigid and there are no clear dividing lines between the different groups. Equally, there is no clear cut off point between people with mild learning disabilities and the general population. It is always helpful to remember that you must see the person first and that labels and categories are ways that individuals and society have sought to identify and plan for particular groups of citizens. The section below concentrates on the medical and social models of disability and this will show that the labels and categories we use have been developed from deep rooted attitudes to people with disabilities.

The continuum of learning ability

In an attempt to explain the wide range of different abilities the idea of a continuum of learning has been used for some time. The terms currently used are shown on the continuum below and are then described in more detail.

Profound – People with profound intellectual and multiple disabilities, or profound and multiple learning disabilities (PMLD), can be some of the most disabled individuals in our communities. They have a profound intellectual disability, which means that their intelligence quotient (IQ) is estimated to be under 20 and therefore they have severely limited understanding (further information about IQ tests can be found on page 8). In addition, they may have multiple disabilities, which can include impairments of vision, hearing and movement as well as other challenges such as epilepsy and autism. Most people in this group need support with mobility and many have complex health needs requiring extensive support. People with profound intellectual and multiple disabilities may have considerable difficulty communicating

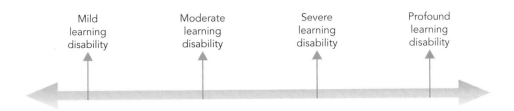

Mild learning disability   Moderate learning disability   Severe learning disability   Profound learning disability

The continuum of learning ability.

and characteristically have very limited understanding. Many people express themselves through non-verbal means, or at most through using a few words or symbols. In addition some people need support with behaviour that is seen as challenging, such as self-injury. There are about 16,000 adults with profound and multiple learning disabilities (PMLD) in England. This definition is taken from the *Raising Our Sights* report (2010) by Professor Jim Mansell.

Severe – People with a severe learning disability often use basic words and gestures to communicate their needs. Many need a high level of support with everyday activities such as cooking, budgeting, cleaning and shopping, but many can look after some if not all of their own personal care needs. Some people have additional medical needs and some need support with mobility issues.

Moderate – People with a moderate learning disability are likely to have some language skills that mean they can communicate about their day to day needs and wishes. People may need some support with caring for themselves, but many will be able to carry out day to day tasks with support.

Mild – A person who is said to have a mild learning disability is usually able to hold a conversation, and communicate most of their needs and wishes. They may need some support to understand abstract or complex ideas. People are often independent in caring for themselves and doing many everyday tasks. They usually have some basic reading and writing skills. People with a mild learning disability quite often go undiagnosed. Most people still need appropriate support with tasks such as budgeting and completing forms.

Using labels for learning disabilities can be both helpful and unhelpful at the same time. It can be helpful to the person, their family or those people who work with them to understand their needs and what support they might need. However, the categories can be unhelpful if the person with the learning disability is just seen as that label, for example 'profound learning disability', and not as 'John'. This can mean that the person is seen as being different to other people or that they get put together with others who have that same label (even though they might have nothing in common with them), or that they don't get opportunities to do things because they are seen as not able to do certain things because of the label. An example would be a person with a learning disability living somewhere where their support staff do everything for them and don't give them the opportunity to use or develop new skills.

People with disabilities have campaigned for many years against being defined by a label using the slogan 'label jars not people'. It is still important to keep this in mind and to always see the person first and foremost and not any label others might use to describe them.

Label jars, not people.

Chapter 2 has more information about the labels we used in the past and Chapter 3 has more information about the implications of having a diagnosis of learning disability.

Intelligence quotient (IQ) tests

Today, assessments of how people can manage with their daily living skills (known as their adaptive function) are considered more useful in assessing the impact of any learning disability on a person than a test of intelligence or IQ. Adaptive function tests tend only to be used when an assessment is required for a specific purpose and are therefore not generally available for every person with a learning disability. What a person can achieve or do doesn't necessarily relate to their IQ score, as it depends on what opportunities they have had to learn and practise living and social skills.

IQ tests are no longer routinely used because their value is questioned by many professionals. However, intelligence testing using IQ tests which produce a numerical score can still be accepted in some medical, educational and legal settings as the basis for confirming a diagnosis of learning disabilities.

An IQ test if needed is administered by a psychologist, to produce an IQ score. This is a statistical score compared with average intelligence which is 100, with 71 to 130 considered to be within the normal range.

An IQ of 70 is an international benchmark of having a learning disability. People with a mild learning disability have an IQ of 50 to 70; which is by far the largest group within the general population, as estimates suggest a prevalence of around 25 per 1000 population (Department of Health 2001). Some individuals with mild learning disabilities may even not be identified because they function and adapt well socially. People with moderate learning disabilities have an IQ of 35 to 50; severe learning disabilities has meant an IQ of 20 to 35; and an IQ of less than 20 puts people in a category of having a profound learning disability. We describe this as the bell shaped distribution of intelligence. The diagram below shows how most people (about 95%) fall within normal range of intelligence and that there are decreasing numbers of people with very high and lower IQs.

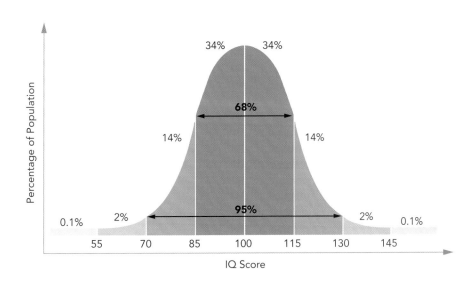

Distribution of intelligence scores.

In the past, people with a learning disability used to be referred to as having a particular mental age, by comparing a person's abilities to a chronological age, for example 'John is 27 but he has a mental age of 4'. This is now seen as inaccurate and insulting, although very occasionally the press still describe people with a learning disability in this way.

Causes of learning disability

A learning disability is lifelong. It is not an illness and cannot be 'cured', and it usually has a considerable impact on a person's life. However, a person's learning disability can have much less impact on their lives when they have the right support. A person with a learning disability can definitely learn new skills and live a full life.

A learning disability can be caused by many things. It is permanent and is present from childhood. The different causes of learning disability are usually put into four categories: before birth, during birth, after birth and multiple causes.

- **Before birth or pre-natal** – this covers genetic causes like Down's syndrome, Fragile X syndrome and also other things that affect a baby before it is born such as drug or alcohol use by the expectant mother.

- **During birth or peri-natal** – this includes lack of oxygen to the baby during birth, which can lead to brain damage. It can include injury to the baby because of complications during birth, and it also includes difficulties resulting from premature birth.

- **After birth or post-natal** – covers causes such as a child having a severe head injury, a serious illness such as meningitis, or suffering from severe neglect. For people with a mild learning disability, social aspects such as overcrowding and poverty together with a lack of developmental opportunities are often important childhood factors.

- **Multiple causes** – this refers to the situation when a person's learning disability is caused by a combination of before, during and after birth factors.

Studies of the causes of learning disabilities

It is important to understand that people don't always know the cause or causes of their learning disability. A number of studies in the 1990s showed that for four out of five children and adults with a severe or profound learning disability, their disability was more likely to have been caused by what the researchers identified as 'biological' factors. These included genetic causes and biological issues before and after birth such as infections, injury or complicating medical conditions. These studies identified that for every five children and adults with a mild learning disability, only between one and two of them could identify a biological cause for their learning disability (Emerson et al. 2001).

Past studies have shown that mild learning disabilities are more strongly associated with the family's social and environmental background. Since these studies there have also been changes in the population of people with a learning disability, for example because people are living longer and because some children with very complex needs are now living into adulthood. Most experts now think that the picture is not as straightforward as these earlier studies indicated.

The medical and social models of disability

These models of disability were developed in the late twentieth century to provide a social and political explanation for how society understands disability and the different attitudes to disabled people, including people with a learning disability.

In **the medical model of disability** the person with a disability is considered to be ill or to have 'something wrong with them'. It describes a school of thought where disabled people should be 'treated', 'cured', 'changed', 'improved' and made more 'normal'. Services that took this approach were traditionally controlled and run by non-disabled people, often in health settings. It was assumed that people with the same label had the same needs and that people should be treated as a group rather than as individuals. Medical practitioners identified therapies and medical interventions to enable people to better fit in with the non-disabled world, and they used their power to control how people lived their lives. This approach has been replaced in the UK and other countries by the social model of disability.

The social model of disability was first described by UPIAS (the Union of Physically Impaired Against Segregation), a group of disability activists, and the term 'social model of disability' was then coined by disabled people. The social model of disability helps us understand the difference between **disability** and **impairment**. **Impairment** means the loss or lack of functioning in a part of the body which results in physical differences or limitations, for example a person who has difficulty hearing has a hearing impairment.

Disability refers to the meaning society attaches to someone who has an impairment, and how they respond to it, and the disadvantage or restriction of activity placed upon people by others which exclude them. For example, a person with a hearing impairment may be disabled by the lack of amplification at a theatre, the lack of provision of sign language interpreters or by people's negative attitudes.

The social model of disability helps us to understand that the barriers to a person living a full and active life are actually part of society, as opposed to being with the person, as in the medical model. The barriers disabled people face can be:

- structural – this can be to do with failures in organisations and social structures;

- environmental – for example, a building not being accessible to people with mobility problems;

- attitudinal – if people have negative attitudes towards disabled people.

The social model of disability emphasises a person's right to be a full citizen and included in all aspects of everyday life. The model identifies and challenges the disabling 'social barriers' in the lives of people with impairments. People with disabilities themselves have changed the way that people now view disability. We now understand the meaning of disability to be about social barriers rather than being about the person's impairment. This means that disability is now seen as a form of social oppression and exclusion that should not be tolerated, just like the oppressions associated with gender, race, class and sexuality.

For people with learning disabilities, the social model of disability means that all of us should focus on people's capabilities and not their deficits, and on what needs to change in society so that people can live their lives to the full. It recognises that people with a learning disability are equal members of society with equal rights and that they have skills, abilities, knowledge and experience.

How many people have a learning disability?

We don't know exactly how many people in the UK have a learning disability. Partly this is because they are not a distinct group of people and there is no clear cut off point between those people with a mild learning disability and those considered not to have a learning disability.

In the past there have been poor records of how many people have a learning disability, although now most local authorities and GP surgeries keep a register. There are now much better local authority registers of children with special needs, so in future years there will be better information about how many adults with a learning disability there might be in an area.

The number, or prevalence, of people with severe and profound learning disability is fairly uniformly distributed across the country and between socio-economic groups. Mild to moderate learning disability is more closely associated with poverty, and rates of learning disability are higher in socially and economically deprived areas.

- In 2001, *Valuing People* estimated that there are roughly 1.4 million people with a learning disability in England.

- This figure is made up of approximately 1.2 million people with a mild or moderate learning disability and 210,000 with a severe or profound learning disability.

- These figures were based on the proposal that about 2% of the general population have a learning disability.

- For the United Kingdom as a whole the figure of 1.5 million people with a learning disability is usually used.

It is thought that the number of people who will have a learning disability in the future will increase. This is because:

- the UK population is expected to increase due to a rise in the birth rate in the next ten years;

- people with a learning disability are living longer because of better medical treatment, better quality of life, food and homes;

- many children who have complex needs are surviving for longer due to better medical treatment.

In a report called *People with Learning Disabilities in England* (Emerson and Hatton 2008) it was estimated that 985,000 people in England have a learning disability (2% of the general population). This figure includes 828,000 adults. The report also estimated that 177,000 adults were known to receive support from learning disability services in England (equivalent to 0.47% of the adult population), which means there are a lot of people who do have a learning disability but do not get services or support.

An excellent source of detailed statistical information on the population of people with a learning disability can be found on this website for the learning disability observatory at www.improvinghealthandlives.org.uk

People from the black and minority ethnic (BME) communities

About 15% of the UK population are from black and minority ethnic communities and these numbers are expected to rise in line with the whole UK population. This is the same for people from BME groups within the learning disability community, and there will be an increase in the proportion of younger adults who belong to South Asian minority ethnic communities, although we don't know exact numbers.

The possible impact of having a family member with a learning disability

Thinking point

Do you have a member of your family who has a learning disability? If yes think about some of the impacts on your family. If you don't have a family member with a learning disability how do you think having a member of the family who has a learning disability might impact on the rest of the family? Think about both positive and negative impacts.

Each family will react in their own way particular way to having a member with a learning disability.

Just as each person with a learning disability is a person in their own right with their own dreams and needs, so too each family is different with their particular priorities and experiences. So each family will react in their own particular way to having a member with a learning disability. Many families that include a person with a learning disability say how much joy and happiness they have brought to the family and how it has enabled them to have a different perspective on life. Family members may feel they have an increased sense of maturity and tolerance, and take great pride in their child's or sibling's accomplishments. Many parents have what they describe as a very special relationship with their child and how they have enriched their lives. For many families, it is their disabled children who keep them going.

> *Paula's mum says:*
>
> Paula has such a strong extrovert personality – it forces people to see her as a person rather than just seeing her disability. It makes it easier for us to cope too – she's a great help to us in that way.

Valuing People Now (2009), the government's three year strategy for services in England, says families are at the heart of the policy. It says, 'When we use the term "family" we are including everyone in the family, including people with learning disabilities. No two families are the same and they come in all shapes and sizes...' You need to remember this when considering the possible impact on a family of having a member with a learning disability.

You can find out more about working in a person centred way and in partnership with family carers in the book *Partnership Working with Family Carers of People with a Learning Disability and People with Autism*, by Alison Cowen and Jamie Hanson, published by BILD.

Below are some other aspects of having a family member with a learning disability that some families tell us they experience:

- The parents may feel guilty – that it was their fault that their child has a learning disability.

- Parents may be unable to work as they have to care for their family member who has a learning disability.

- This could lead to the stress of having less money, trying to 'make ends meet' as they are now living off benefits.

- There is also stress on other relationships in the family as there is less time to spend with other family members.

- Family carers may have little or no time for themselves.

- Carers may feel physically or emotionally tired living with someone who has complex needs.

- Carers may feel isolated because they get little or no support from professionals or time to meet their own friends.

- Black and minority ethnic community families say there can be an assumption by professionals that the extended family will provide the required support, which may not be the case.

Many carers do not know that support is available for them. Family members say that access to information, financial support and being able to have breaks are all important in helping them manage the effect of caring on their lives. If you have details about local and national carer support services make sure that these are available to the family carers that you know.

> *One family describes how they feel about having to fight for services – the mother of a young man with Down's syndrome says:*
>
> I don't feel 'why me?' – after all – 'why not?' – but more a sense that other people, including service providers, lack a perception of what caring is all about. When this happens I find myself wishing yet again that it hadn't happened to our family.

Family members are often the 'experts' on the person with a learning disability as they know them better than anyone. However, many family members often feel that their knowledge and skills aren't welcomed by professionals who sometimes think that they know what is best for the person who has a learning disability. You can help to address this by listening carefully to the views of family carers and treating them with dignity and respect.

Key points from this chapter

- People with learning disabilities are equal people with the same rights as everyone else and should be treated with dignity and respect.

- People with learning disabilities are always people first and it is important to always focus on what the person can do rather than what they can't.

- Learning disability can be seen as part of a continuum of learning abilities.

- The medical model of disability describes people with a learning disability as having an illness that needs to be cured.

- The social model of disability says that it is barriers in society that are the cause of discrimination against people with a learning disability. Some of the barriers to people with a learning disability being treated as equal citizens include people's attitudes, their lack of understanding and respect.

- Although our knowledge has increased, our understanding of the many causes of learning disability is still limited.

- Family carers are often the 'expert' on their family member who has a learning disability.

References and where to go for more information

References

Cowen, A and Hanson, J (2012) *Partnership Working with Family Carers of People with a Learning Disability and People with Autism.* Kidderminster: BILD

Emerson, E and Hatton, C (2004) *Estimating the Current Need/ Demand for Support for People with a Learning Disability.* Institute of Health Research Lancaster University, downloadable from www.improvinghealthandlives.org.uk

Emerson, E et al. (2001) *Learning Disabilities: the fundamental facts*. London: Foundation for People with Learning Disabilities

Mansell, J (2010) *Raising our Sights: Services for adults with profound intellectual and multiple disabilities*. University of Kent, Tizard Centre

Rolph, S, Atkinson, D, Nind, M, and Welshman, J. (2005) *Witnesses to Change: Families, learning difficulties and history*. Kidderminster: BILD

Legislation, policies and reports

Department of Health (2001) *Valuing People: A New Strategy for Learning Disability for the 21st Century – a White Paper*. London: Department of Health

Department of Health (2009) *Valuing People Now*. London: Department of Health

Websites

BILD www.bild.org.uk

Contact a Family www.cafamily.org.uk

Foundation for People with Learning Disabilities: www.learningdisabilities.org.uk

Improving Health and Lives: Learning Disability Health Observatory www.improvinghealthandlives.org.uk

Mencap www.mencap.org.uk

People First www.peoplefirstltd.com

PMLD Network www.pmldnetwork.org

University of Bristol, Norah Fry Centre www.bris.ac.uk/cipold

Valuing People www.valuingpeoplenow.dh.gov.uk

Chapter 2

Understanding the historical context of learning disability

I remember when the centre used to be an adult training centre, where I did contract work, and I feel this was slave labour as I got paid £2 a week, which was rubbish.

Janet

There have been marked improvements in the lives and circumstances of adults with learning disabilities in the 30 years between the 1971 White Paper *Better Services for the Mentally Handicapped* and its successor document *Valuing People*. As Ivan Lewis MP, a past Minister of State for Care Services, reminded us: 'On the whole the closure of the long stay mental handicap hospitals was a success and was of great credit to all those involved ...' As a result, many fewer people now live in long stay institutions, segregated away from the rest of society. Many more live in ordinary housing in the community. A minority have paid jobs... Noticeable too is the number of people with learning disabilities who are active in self advocacy groups, speaking their views and getting their voice heard ... something that was unheard of 30 years ago... But this picture of positive change has been recently tarnished by a string of reports and inquiries which have revealed a darker, and more shocking, side of life for some adults with learning disabilities in the 21st century.

A Life Like Any Other? Human rights of adults with learning disabilities (2008)

Learning outcomes

This chapter will help you to:

- explain the types of support and services that have been provided for people with learning disabilities in the past;

- describe how past ways of working may affect present support and services;

- outline the key changes in the following areas of the lives of individuals who have learning disabilities:

  - where people live;

  - daytime activity;

  - employment;

  - sexual relationships and parenthood;

  - the provision of healthcare;

  - the introduction of self-directed support.

This chapter covers:

Level 2 LD 201 – Understand the context of supporting individuals with learning disabilities: Learning Outcome 3

Introduction

Many of us use the phrase 'that is history repeating itself' when we see the same thing happening again and again. Unfortunately, when we say this we often mean that we haven't learnt from what happened in the past and both good and bad things are repeating themselves. When people heard recently of more reported cases of abuse of people with a learning disability many thought this was 'history repeating itself'.

In this chapter you will find out about how people with a learning disability have lived their lives and been supported in the past and how their support has changed and developed over the last 150 years. Today many people with learning disabilities live in their own home, have a job and lead active lives in their local community. This is a big improvement from the past when many people lived in large long stay hospitals and residential homes and where people had little privacy and lived institutional lives.

However, many people still don't have a home of their own or a job, and they can lead lonely and isolated lives. If you are to make sense of the experiences of the people you support and their families then you need to have an understanding of how people lived and were supported in the past. In particular we need to learn from the real stories of people with a learning disability and their families. Over the last 30 years there has been a growth in documenting the stories and experiences of people with a learning disability and their families. This is an important and rich source of information, and we can learn so much from what has happened in their lives and experiences.

Past support and services for people with a learning disability

Nineteenth century support

In the pre-industrial period of British history, before the nineteenth century, the majority of the population lived in rural settings or in small villages or towns and were employed on the land or in handcrafts. People lived in small communities and most knew their neighbours. In these situations, people with disabilities were part of their local community. There is some historical evidence that people were 'well integrated into their communities, many of them working, while those who were too disabled to work were supported by families and friends'. However, 'the harshness of the period should not be underestimated – language to describe people with disabilities is direct and to the modern ears, insulting. It is clear that many people suffered bullying, teasing and worse in the workplace and on the streets, and sexual and physical abuse were common' (Jarrett 2010).

The asylum for idiots at Earlswood Common, Redhill, Surrey.

With the growth of factories as part of the industrial revolution, an increasing number of people moved from the country to the towns. Communities changed as they became larger and more anonymous. Many people lived in poor housing and worked long hours for poor pay. Factory work brought considerable changes to how people managed their lives and homes. People had to work long hours, with regular clocking on and off times and employers requiring high levels of productivity from their workers. In these changing situations many people with disabilities found it more difficult to contribute in the more regulated environment. People with disabilities were less likely to find work in factories, particularly if they weren't as productive as their non disabled colleagues. In addition, as most of the family, including children, were away from the home working there was less support for people at home. It was as a response to this new social and working environment that segregated support for people with a range of disabilities developed.

This was supported by legislation including the Lunatic Asylums Act (1853) which compelled every county and borough to provide an asylum 'for the pauper lunatics in the district and every person being an idiot'. The new asylums and institutions for people with mental health needs and people with learning disabilities began to develop from the 1840s onwards. The early asylums were normally funded by local communities and entrepreneurs. The word 'asylum' means 'place of safety' and their development was seen as a positive response to changing social situations.

The 1886 Idiots Act encouraged local authorities to build asylums for 'idiots, imbeciles and the feeble minded' and so take them out of the workhouse and the asylums for lunatics. This began the separation between people with mental health needs and people with a learning disability.

In the late nineteenth century there was a rise in the popularity of the eugenics movement, which focused on the science of improving the human race by controlling inherited characteristics. Supporters of this cause raised concerns about what they saw as increasing numbers of people with disabilities, who were wrongly portrayed as obsessed with sex or as criminals. The views of some of those who supported the eugenics movement captured the thinking at the time:

> Idiots are one rank of that fearful host which is ever pressing upon society with its suffering, its miseries and its crimes and which society is ever trying to hold off at arm's length – to keep in quarantine, to shut up in jails or almshouses, or at least to train as a pariah caste: but all in vain.

Samuel Howe

We must control this wandering population of mental defective persons who are many of them dangerous, morally and physically, and criminal in their characteristics

Royal Commission on the Care of the Feeble-minded 1904–1908

The eugenics movement in the United Kingdom continued to have considerable influence until the outbreak of the Second World War in 1939. This led to the growth in the number of asylums and compulsory detention for many people with a learning disability. In addition many women with a learning disability were compulsorily sterilised.

The 1913 Mental Deficiency Act used the term mental deficiency to define the condition of learning disability as 'existing from birth or early age'. The Act defined four categories of mental defective: idiots, feeble minded people, imbeciles and moral defectives. A moral defective was often a woman who had become pregnant and was unmarried. Once people were labelled and sent to an asylum or other institution, it was extremely difficult for them to leave or be discharged. The asylums became the long term homes for most people with a learning disability. Segregation became the inevitable response to the concerns expressed by the eugenics movement.

The Second World War was a watershed. In Germany, Adolf Hitler had embraced the eugenics movement and a central part of his strategy was to produce the 'pure Aryan race'. This drove his Nazi party to kill many people with disabilities in Germany prior to his 'final solution', the Holocaust. Hitler's actions were seen as the consequence of the eugenics movement and it's hardly surprising that this approach was completely discredited by the end of the war in 1945.

After the Second World War

At the end of the war there was considerable optimism as the rebuilding of the country began. The welfare state was created and the National Health Service came into being in 1948. As part of this initiative all of the asylums became hospitals and were included in the National Health Service. Although this could be seen as a positive breakthrough, there were negative impacts on the lives of people with a learning disability in the new hospitals.

Calling the asylums hospitals created tensions as normally people only go to hospital when they are sick. Having received treatment, people are usually discharged as they have been made well again. People with a learning disability are not 'sick', their condition is lifelong and cannot be cured. However, the long stay hospitals were staffed by consultant psychiatrists, doctors and nurses, and the individuals living there were viewed as patients who needed treatment. This medical approach gave individuals few choices or decisions and they were often prescribed medication as a means of control.

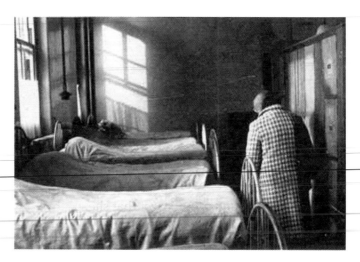

In the long stay hospitals people lived in crowded wards with few personal possessions.

In the long stay hospitals, people often lived on large crowded wards with very few possessions. Clothes were often shared out when they returned from the laundry. Staffing levels were often very low which meant that care and support were provided through institutional practices, especially at meal times and bath times. Strict routines were followed and there was no allowance for individual choice. There was little privacy and men and women were rarely allowed to mix. There was limited family contact.

During the years of the asylums and hospitals families very often had no say in the way in which their baby, child or young person was removed and sent to the long stay hospital. Quite often parents were told to 'go away, forget about their child and try for another baby'.

In learning about the eugenics movement and the way in which people were segregated and locked away in the long stay hospitals, it is important to think about the impact that this had on families. Today older family carers who have spent their lives caring for their son or daughter will be aware of the public perceptions that mirrored the hospital provision. When the closure of the hospitals started to take place in the 1970s and 1980s many family carers who had been told the hospital was the only place for their relative then had to cope emotionally with their move out into community care.

In her book Caring for Kathleen *(2000), Peggy Fray explains about what happened to her family in the 1920s when her sister Kathleen was born with Down's syndrome:*

At the time of her birth there was no welfare state... our own mother was advised in 1927 to put her daughter into an institution and try to forget that she had been born... When the children (with learning disabilities) live at home, it has usually been the case that the carers made such a good job of the caring that it has not been considered that much help is needed – often to the great detriment of the health of all concerned.

Peggy and Kathleen.

The slow progress towards better support and services started with the 1959 Mental Health Act. This legislation:

- removed the terms idiot, imbecile, feeble minded and moral defective and replaced them with mental sub normality and severe sub normality;

- lessened the hospital's powers of detention, although many people stayed as voluntary patients as they had nowhere left to go and were not told they could leave;

- encouraged local authorities to start providing residential hostels or homes and day services then adult training centres.

The demise of the long stay hospitals occurred not because of policy guidance but as a response to a series of abuse scandals which started at Ely Hospital Cardiff in 1969. When the spotlight was turned towards what was happening in the long stay hospitals it was inevitable that this approach would be discredited. This led to an emphasis on community care, with people with a learning disability being supported to live and build links and networks in their local communities.

The 1971 White Paper *Better Services for the Mentally Handicapped* stimulated the start of the resettlement programme where people moved out of the long stay hospitals to live in their local community. There was a growth in community based hostels and residential homes as well as local authority day services. Services were provided by local authorities and a growing voluntary sector. A number of charities that still provide support for people with a learning disability were leading the growth of community based support. A number of charities were set up by family carers motivated by the need for good local support for their family member.

In the 1970s more residential homes opened for people with a learning disability.

For more information about the role of families in providing support and services from the 1940s onwards the book *Witnesses to Change – families, learning difficulties and history* (2005) by Sheena Rolph and others is very useful.

New ideas of normalisation and social role valorisation

Normalisation is the idea or social theory that 'non-valued' people will become 'normal' if we treat them like the rest of society. It was introduced by Wolf Wolfensberger in the 1980s in America and soon after came to Britain. Community integration was at the core of this philosophy, which drove the deinstitutionalisation movement. This was later developed into Social Role Valorisation or SRV, a theory based on the idea that society tends to identify groups of people as fundamentally 'different', and of less value than everyone else. SRV suggests that attention should be given to changing poor attitudes by helping people with disabilities to take on valued social roles, for example as family members, neighbours, employees, etc.

The principle of an ordinary life

One of the outcomes of normalisation in the UK was the vision of *An Ordinary Life* promoted by the Kings Fund. Their *An Ordinary Life* initiative, launched in 1980, was instrumental in the ways in which services and support developed in the rest of the 1980s and beyond — people with learning disabilities living ordinary lives in ordinary houses in their local communities. This was in stark contrast to the institutional experiences that many had been subjected to previously. *An Ordinary Working Life* was published in 1984 and focused on people having real jobs, leading to the development of supported employment programmes and initiatives. These principles had a huge impact on how services were planned and delivered in the subsequent years.

An ordinary life meant living in an ordinary house in a local community.

The hospital and NHS campus closure programme has taken over 40 years to complete, with the final closure of these settings only happening in 2011. However, the recent growth of private sector hospitals and assessment and treatment units has meant that this type of support is still not a thing of the past.

As the long stay hospitals closed, many people were moved into residential homes. Most were large, catering for groups of over 20 people. This meant that individuals would be living with people that they didn't know and might not even like. People were often selected to live together, because they had similar needs or because there were limited choices where people could live. These homes or hostels as they were sometimes called were still not set up to meet individual needs and choices so in effect they turned into 'mini-institutions'.

David says:

When I was four years old I was admitted to a hospital for adults and children in the north of England because my mother couldn't cope and I was having lots of fits. I spent my childhood there. I rarely saw my family as it was hard for them to visit. I had nothing of my own; toys, clothing and even shoes were shared. I had no space of my own and no control in my life.

At 18 I left the hospital to move to my family home because the welfare people said my bed was needed. I found this hard as I wanted to go back to the hospital. I felt it was my home and didn't know any different.

I've spent my life living at home with my family, in various hostels and group homes, adult placements and supported living. I had little choice and never felt settled.

Life's different now. 18 months ago I got my own flat! I love it! This was the result of the staff actually listening to what I wanted, and working hard to make it happen. It wasn't an easy journey. But now I can do what I want when I want, I have support to complete the rota of those supporting me and I choose when I have that support.

This is it now, I can live my life!

With thanks to MacIntyre for this story

Learning disability support and services in Britain in the late nineteenth and twentieth century. Table of major developments (adapted from Forgotten Lives: exploring the history of learning disability (2003) and from website Unlocking the past at www.unlockingthepast.org.uk)

Date	Legislation and national events	Major developments	Professional, parent and advocacy groups	Changing labels
1601	Poor Law Act	Parish poor houses developed for poor, sick and older people		
1845	Lunacy Act had muddled definitions of learning disability and mental illness	Regional asylums set up specifically for children and adults with learning disabilities		Muddled distinctions 'lunatics shall mean insane person or any person being idiot or lunatic or of unsound mind'
1886	Idiots Act made clear the distinction between lunatics and 'idiots' and 'imbeciles'	Ongoing development of asylums and institutions, funded by local communities and philanthropists		Introduced the terms lunatics, idiots and imbeciles
1908 Report of the Royal Commission on the Care and Control of the Feeble-minded	1902 Sandlebridge Colony opened 1907 Formation of the Eugenics Education Society	Growth of regional asylums or institutions		

Date	Legislation and national events	Major developments	Professional, parent and advocacy groups	Changing labels
1913	1913 Mental Deficiency Act 1914 Elementary Education Act	The state became involved in the running of the asylums and institutions		Use of the diagnostic terms 'idiot', 'feeble minded', 'imbecile' and 'moral imbecile' in the 1913 Act
1927	1927 Mental Deficiency (Amendment) Act			'moral defective' replaced 'moral imbecile'
1930s	Campaign for Voluntary Sterilisation	More colonies opened for 'mental defectives' 1934 Brock report recommends sterilisation		
1940s	1944 Education Act 1948 NHS Act	NHS took over institutions and asylums as hospitals Late 1940s major expansion of training (day) centres	Mental welfare officers appointed to support people outside of hospitals 1946 Association of Parents of Backward Children founded (later Mencap)	Use of the term 'sub normal' started in USA

1950s	Royal Commission on Mental Health 1959 Mental Health Act	Growth of village communities Local authorities started to provide residential homes and hostels	1959 Mental Health Act used the terms 'subnormal' and 'severely subnormal'
1960s	Department of Health says mental sub normality hospitals to close in 15 years Hospital abuse scandals at Ely, Farleigh, South Ockendon and Normansfield	Developing work on integration and normalisation began to affect professionals, policies and services	
1970s	1971 Better Services for the Mentally Handicapped 1970 Education Act makes education universal	Beginning of closure of long stay hospitals and growth of large hostels and residential homes Growth of community day centres All children with learning disabilities entitled to an education; no longer seen as ineducable 1972 Wolf Wolfensberger's *Principles of Normalisation* published in Canada	BILD started work as the Institute of Mental Sub normality National Development Team in Department of Health supported local and regional changes to services

1980s	1981 Education Act aimed to integrate children with a learning disability into ordinary schools 1983 Mental Health Act aimed to provide support in the community as far as possible; no compulsory admission of people with learning disabilities unless their disability was associated with severe mental health or behavioural needs 1983 All Wales Strategy for development of services to mentally handicapped people	Ongoing work to close hospitals; development of community care and the growth of group homes An Ordinary Life published by King's Fund advocating normalisation	Growth of self advocacy movement	People with 'mental handicap' became the preferred term from about 1980
1990s	1991 NHS Community Act said the lead agency for people with learning disabilities to be the local authority and not the NHS. An individual assessment of need leading to the funding of a care package Disability Discrimination Act 1995	Ongoing work to close hospitals and develop local community support Development of a range of services by health services, local authorities and a growth of the private for profit and voluntary sector Development of person centred planning in the USA and UK influenced the growth of individualised support for people	Mencap celebrate 50 years First 'People First' conference of self advocates	The term 'learning disabilities' introduced to replace 'mental handicap' by Department of Health Self advocates say they prefer the term 'learning difficulties'

Details about the more recent legislation and policies that are influencing current support for people with a learning disability can be found in Chapter 6.

Labels

As you can see from the table above people with a learning disability have been given many different labels over the years. Many of the labels were originally formal terms of medical diagnosis, but they later became derogatory or slang terms. They show us how people with a learning disability were viewed in the past.

Even in recent years the term mental deficiency was in general use and then we referred to people as mentally handicapped. People with a learning disability were also referred to as 'backward'. You can imagine these labels have not been helpful to enabling people to be accepted as equal citizens.

A series of campaigns including from the People First movement changed this term to 'people with a mental handicap' in the 1980s. This was to encourage and remind everyone that people with a learning disability are people first. This was used until the term 'learning disability' was first used and then adopted by the Department of Health in 1992.

Special education

Until the Education of Handicapped Children Act in 1970, some children with learning disabilities were considered uneducable and so attended junior training centres. Following the Act the responsibility for all children with learning disabilities moved from health authorities to the education authorities. Children were labelled ESN (M) (educationally sub-normal – mild) or ESN (S) (severe) on the basis of assessment and those with profound and multiple learning disabilities went to a 'special care unit'. This means that some older people with a learning disability have never been to school.

From the 1990s many more children with disabilities started going to mainstream schools with individual support. However, many children continue to go to special schools and receive segregated education from the age of three to nineteen.

How learning from the past can lead to improved support

Positive impacts on current support

You can see from this brief history that lessons have been learned and changes made in the support that society has provided for people with a learning disability. Now, policies have changed away from institutionalised care to person-centred support, that is support and services to meet each individual's needs, choices and decisions. Services aim to enable people to have full and meaningful lives including relationships and friendships together with an acknowledgement of people's emotional and spiritual needs. In addition, the importance of access to all forms of advocacy is recognised and people are supported to speak up for themselves and have their views listened to.

Most people with a learning disability use fewer segregated services and are more included in the communities where they live. We recognise that people's identities are much more than their learning disability and that this also includes culture, race, faith and sexuality. People with learning disabilities are now recognised as equal members of society with equal rights that are protected in law.

Many pieces of legislation, guidance policies and procedures have been produced to promote good practice and there is better training and improved qualification structures for staff. For more information on current policies that influence support for people with a learning disability please go to Chapter 6. We now recognise that it is important that people with a learning disability have love, joy, hope and laughter in their lives.

Negative impacts on current support

However, for all the good work that has been done and the positive impact of past experiences on current support, there are still negative ways of working that persist to this day, including:

- Old ways of working were in place for hundreds of years – so it is difficult to change all of the old attitudes overnight.

- Some organisations are still institutionalised in their approach, putting the smooth running of the service before the needs of the people they support.

- Some organisations work by a medical model of disability and not the social model.

- Some organisations don't have systems in place to support staff to do their job well and confidently, e.g. supervision and appraisals. Many organisations have policies and procedures in place, for example on safeguarding and protection, but not all of their staff know about these or follow them when they need to.

- Not everyone believes people with a learning disability are able to make their own decisions and so limit their choices and opportunities.

- Family carers are not listened to and respected.

Changes in the lives of people with a learning disability

From asylums to a home of your own

Today the majority of adults with a learning disability still live with their families in the family home. Some people stay in the family home until their parents become elderly and need care themselves. Their family carers provide a lot of their support as well as the love and care that goes with being part of a family. It is important to understand the needs of family carers and the significance of their caring role on their life experience. More information on supporting older carers can be found at www.lifetimecaring.org.uk

After the closure of the larger institutions, the people who were unable to live with their families were often moved to live in hostels, residential care or nursing homes. A few moved to their own home either with a tenancy or a mortgage. This meant that people tended to live in a home belonging to the council, or a private or voluntary sector organisation, rather than their own home. At the same time the support staff were often provided by the same organisation or by the council.

Over the last 20 years there has been a decline in the number of people living in residential and nursing homes and an increase in the number of people living in their own home with support from staff from a domiciliary care provider. Housing Options is a national housing advisory service that provides information for people with learning disability and others about a range of housing choices. For more information go to www.housingoptions.org.uk

When people live in their own home either as a tenant or a home owner, they have more security and protection in law. In addition, they can also more easily change how they are supported without needing to change where they live. They can do this by receiving their support from a different provider. Individuals may live on their own with one or two friends with learning disabilities or have a tenancy on their own or with a partner. When people have their own individual budgets, they can employ their own personal assistants to support them so they can have greater flexibility in determining the how and when of their support.

Many people live in their own home, either as a tenant or a home owner.

From day centres to employment

Some people with learning disabilities still attend day centres, but these have changed a lot in the last ten years. In the past such services provided activities and occupation for people, during the day. Many people attending a day centre lived at home with their family and five days' attendance at a day service provided families with a break from caring. In the 1940s and 1950s there was a focus on preparation for employment and an opportunity to practise work tasks in a sheltered environment. Services then developed a therapeutic emphasis as the number of people with complex needs increased. In the last 20 years the focus has been on using day centres as a base within the local community for people to meet and then go out and about using community facilities. Activities are now provided to develop their skills and meet their needs rather than just to occupy people.

Increasingly people with learning disabilities are being supported to participate in community groups, and to use local facilities such as the sports centre and adult education classes. There are increasing opportunities to contribute and to be a local volunteer and this enables people to get to know others in their community rather than just joining groups that are only for people with learning disabilities.

Frances

Frances is a volunteer for a parents and toddlers group at a local church three mornings a week. She makes teas and coffees for the adults and toast for the children, and she helps to put the toys out. She has made new friends doing this and it is a really important part of her week. She loves the way the other volunteers treat her as 'one of them' and her reliable attendance is really appreciated.

Employment

Since the publication of the Department of Health policies for England, *Valuing People Now* (2009) and *Valuing Employment Now* (2010), there has been a greater commitment to supporting more people with a learning disability to find and keep paid employment. Currently only 10% of people with a learning disability of working age are in employment, but 65% want to work. You can find out more information about supporting people with learning disabilities into work at www.base-uk.org. More social enterprises are developing, run by or for people with a learning disability, such as community cafés, horticulture projects and furniture restoration workshops.

Some further education colleges provide courses which people with learning disabilities can go on, to develop their skills, for which they can achieve a qualification. However, these opportunities are reducing due to changes in funding.

Only 7% of adults with a learning disability who are known to social services are in paid employment. However, increasing employment opportunities are a focus in all of the UK's learning disability plans so that more people with learning disabilities have the opportunity to have a 'real job' which helps them to develop skills and confidence, earn a working wage and meet new people. Some people with learning disabilities will need support to do this, but the right support can ensure that they succeed and do a great job. Some people with a learning disability have been able to set up their own businesses or take part in a social enterprise.

There is now a greater commitment to supporting people with a learning disability to find and keep paid employment.

Many local authorities fund a service to enable people with a severe learning disability to find either work experience or paid jobs, and provide them with support to meet all of the requirements of their job. The government has specific programmes to support people with disabilities to gain employment. Access to Work helps people whose health or disability affects the way they do their job. It gives advice and support with extra costs which may arise because of a person's needs. Access to Work might pay towards a support worker or the equipment needed at work, or pay towards the cost of getting to work if someone cannot use public transport.

Work Choice helps people with disabilities whose needs cannot be met through other work programmes, Access to Work or workplace adjustments. This might be because they need more specialised support to find employment or keep a job once they have started work. Work Choice is tailored to meet individual needs. It focuses on helping people achieve their full potential and move towards being more independent, it also gives employers the support they need to employ more disabled people.

> *Steven says:*
>
> We are very much in demand and always have to turn work down! We have to follow clear guidelines because of health and safety and because we are being paid by our customers to do a good job. So in the mornings we have to change into our work clothes and put our boots on. Then after loading the trailers with all the equipment we need for the job we get on the bus and set off to do our first garden. I use a pictorial checklist to make sure that I am wearing the right clothes and have put the right equipment in the trailer.
>
> *Steven is 26 years old and has worked at Grass Routes in Chesterfield for almost five years. Grass Routes is a business that provides gardening services and has contracts to look after 60 community gardens over a two week rota.*
>
> *With thanks to MacIntyre for this story.*
>
> For more information about Steven and about employment opportunities and support go to www.base-uk.org

Friendships, sexual relationships and parenthood

> *Patty*
>
> Patty used to live in a house where she was not allowed to have pets. Now she lives in a house where she can, and so she chose to have a rabbit. Both of the two friends that she lives with and her support workers help to care for him. Having her pet enriches her life and has helped her to develop new friendships.
>
> *With thanks to MacIntyre for this story*

Everyone needs friends, some close special friends and a wider network of acquaintances. People with a learning disability are no different. Our friends and relationships are essential for our wellbeing; we thrive best when we are in interdependent relationships.

Most people with learning disabilities have relationships with family and with the staff that support them, and with others who use the same services as they do. However, some individuals may not always be supported to develop relationships with people who are not paid to be with them.

Rosie says:

My name is Rosie. Myself and Mary my best friend grew up together in Kent. Unfortunately at a young age Mary went to another school and I moved with my family to Staffordshire. We really missed each other but carried on with our new lives.

In 1989 I moved to Milton Keynes to a supported living set up where Mary was already living. I was nervous about meeting Mary again but also very excited. She came to find me. We were so emotional at being reunited but very happy!

Since then we have been best friends. We do lots together. We both enjoy attending Weightwatchers, going to the cinema, theatre and popping out for coffee and a chat. Most importantly we are there for each other to share the happy times and to comfort each other when we're upset.

Having Mary as a friend means the world to me.

With thanks to MacIntyre for this story

In the past, people with a learning disability were often denied having more intimate personal relationships. It was believed that they would only be able to relate to other people with a learning disability and unfortunately their segregated lives meant that they were unable to meet many people who were not paid to support them. Nowadays many people have lots of friends, some of whom have a disability and some do not.

Thinking point

Reflect on your own memories around your personal relationships. You don't have to write the details down, just think through some of the important things that have happened.

Below is a list of things that you may have thought of (in no particular order!)

First boyfriend/girlfriend	*Getting married/civil partnership*
First date	*Having a baby*
First kiss	*Getting divorced*
First time your heart was broken	*Getting re-married*
First time you had sex	*Breaking up and making up*
Getting engaged	*Having grandchildren*
Moving in together	*Celebrating your 25th wedding anniversary*

All too often people with learning disabilities are still denied the opportunity to be involved in a sexual relationship with another person. Sometimes this is because those around them are trying to protect them from harm and risk. However, this approach denies the person their rights and their need for social and personal relationships. Denying these opportunities can be due to:

- negative attitudes;

- ignorance;

- a lack of privacy;

- fear of the person becoming a parent;

- concerns about capacity to consent.

Historically people with learning disabilities have not had their relationships taken seriously; they have been seen as unable to cope with a 'proper' relationship unlike other adult members of society.

Jean says:

I have been in a relationship with Jack for 27 years. I am engaged to Jack. We have known each other since school but then started seeing each other when we went to the same day centre. I would like to see more of Jack, on an evening, going to the pub or for meals etc., the same as other couples do. I see Jack on my birthday and occasionally I get invited to go out with him and his family on his birthday.

I feel frustrated as I feel that we are independent adults, who are grown up and not children, and I feel having a label of 'learning disability' has stopped me and Jack having the opportunity to live together or get married.

Paul says:

I used to have a girlfriend when I went to college, but I no longer see her as I don't go to college. She wanted more from the relationship than I did as she would have liked sex but my Mum wasn't happy for this to happen.

Whilst Jean's and Paul's stories show us that these restricting attitudes can still affect the development of relationships for people with learning disabilities, things are changing for the better. People with learning disabilities who have the capacity to understand the consequences of their own decisions have the same rights to have relationships as every other member of society including the right to marry and have children.

We all have the right to a private and family life, and to marry.

There is a growing awareness that we need to ensure that people with learning difficulties are supported to develop relationships, including sexual ones. However, gay, lesbian and bisexual people with learning difficulties may have additional needs or face particular barriers in this area of their lives, including prejudice and discrimination in the wider society, as well as from staff, services, family and friends.

In the past, women with a learning disability were often sterilised to prevent any risk of unwanted pregnancies or because it was seen to be 'the right thing to do'. All too often women with a learning disability were not given information in a way they could understand and were not fully involved in the decision making. They didn't realise that they would not be able to have a baby after the operation. This cannot happen today without a formal assessment of a person's capacity using the relevant legislation for the country they live in. People are also protected by the Human Rights Act. You can find out more about women's experiences of sterilisation in podcasts from the Open University learning disability history group at www.open.ac.uk/hsc/ldsite/

Parents with learning disabilities

With support people with learning disabilities can be successful parents. However, many have been denied the right to have a child as it has been assumed that they would be unable to cope. Most parents who don't have a learning disability need support of some kind or another, from family or friends, to help them go to work or to have a social life. It is now recognised that parents with a learning disability may need support in their parenting role, such as how to meet the changing developmental needs of their child. They might need to be given information about childcare in a different way so they can understand it and put it into practice. Just because the parents have a learning disability, it does not mean that their children will have a disability. The parents who cope the best are usually the ones with very supportive family and friends, and where they have lots of positive role models. Sometimes parents only need support in the first few years, while other parents might need to have support until their child grows up. Each family's need for support will be different; for some it will be how to play with the children, while for others it might be how to set routines and boundaries, or learning to cook nutritious meals.

> *Sam is a mum with a learning disability; she has a son who is now 20. She says:*
>
> Being a mum is brilliant! I'm really proud of him.

The provision of healthcare

Many people with learning disabilities have had their health needs neglected and overlooked. There are many reasons for this, including a lack of understanding of learning disabilities by healthcare staff, the challenges of communication and the failure of some health services to make reasonable adjustments to meet the needs of disabled people.

People with a learning disability have more health care needs than the general population, but they use health services less. There are higher rates of epilepsy, visual and hearing impairments, psychiatric illness and obesity in people with a learning disability compared with the general population. About 50% of people with a learning disability will have at least one significant health problem; 25% will have a physical disability, and 30% will have epilepsy. These are often long term conditions for which people need ongoing healthcare support.

There have been a number of reports and investigations into the poor healthcare experienced by people with a learning disability. These include:

- **Treat Me Right!**

  This report and campaign by Mencap in 2004 exposed the unequal healthcare that people with a learning disability often receive from healthcare professionals. The report made clear that much work needed to be done within the NHS to ensure that people with a learning disability are treated decently and equally.

  After the launch of the *Treat Me Right!* campaign, many cases of appalling treatment of people with a learning disability in hospitals around the country have come to light.

- **Death by Indifference**

  This report by Mencap (2007) followed on from *Treat Me Right!* It described the untimely deaths of six people with a learning disability in NHS care. Their families were not getting answers as to why their loved ones had died, or whether they were treated so badly because they had a learning disability. It raised serious concerns about the way people with a learning disability are treated within our healthcare system.

- **Healthcare for All – the Michael Report (2008)**

  As a result of the *Death by Indifference* report, an independent inquiry led by Sir Jonathan Michael was carried out, which made recommendations for change to give people with a learning disability equal access to healthcare. The report said:

  > Parents and carers of adults and children with learning disabilities often find their opinions and assessments ignored by healthcare professionals, even though they often have the best information about, and understanding of, the people they support. They struggle to be accepted as effective partners in care by those involved in providing general healthcare; their complaints are not heard; they are expected to do too much of the care that should be provided by the health system and are often required to provide care beyond their personal resources.

  Healthcare for All – Michael Report

The report gave ten recommendations to be implemented by all NHS bodies by 2011.

- **Our Health, Our Care, Our Say**

  Our Health, Our Care, Our Say (Department of Health 2006) made a commitment to providing regular comprehensive health checks to people with learning disabilities, which are recognised as identifying previously undiagnosed health issues and so contributing to improving health.

- **Valuing People (2001) and Valuing People Now (2009)**

  Valuing People (2001) and *Valuing People Now* (2009) identified that improved health care for people was a key outcome. The reports state that all people with learning disabilities have the right to access mainstream health services, and be registered with a GP, and have health action plans. The aim of health action plans is that the individual health needs of all people with learning disabilities are both understood and acted upon.

A health action plan is a personalised plan that identifies the health needs of a person with a learning disability and how these should be met. It is a confidential record which can support the person to manage their own health needs; it is also a valuable reference both for support staff and all health professionals. It identifies which healthcare services and professionals are needed to make sure people have the support to stay healthy.

Healthcare workers need specialist training so that they understand about people with learning disabilities and how to communicate effectively.

> *Janet says:*
>
> My sister usually goes to the GP with me, but I make my own appointments to go to the dentist and I find the staff there are friendly and helpful, I also make appointments and attend the optician on my own and this is fine. I recently went to the walk in centre on my own to have my ears syringed and I was fine about this too.

Key points from this chapter

- Present day attitudes towards people with a learning disability are rooted in how they were treated in the past.

- Past services for people with a learning disability have left a negative legacy of segregated, institutionalised care that focused on the smooth running of the organisation at the expense of the needs of the individual. Even today some isolated services still provide institutionalised care.

References and where to go for more information

References

Abbott, D and Howarth, J (2007) *Secret Loves, Hidden Lives? Exploring issues for people with learning difficulties who are gay, lesbian or bisexual.* Bristol: The Policy Press

Atkinson, D, Jackson, M et al. (1997) *Forgotten Lives: Exploring the history of learning disability.* Kidderminster: BILD

Brend, M (2008) *First and Last: Closing learning disabilities hospitals.* London: Choice Support.

Brigham, L (2000) *Crossing Boundaries: Change and continuity in the history of learning disability.* Kidderminster: BILD

Cowen, A and Hanson, J (2012) *Partnership Working with Family Carers of People with a Learning Disability and People with Autism.* Kidderminster: BILD

Jarrett, S (2010) *'He is a poor and foolish lad.' Before there were staff – informal family and social networks of support in 18th and early 19th century London, How the asylum system broke them up.* Paper abstract from www.open.ac.uk/hsc/ldsite

Kings Fund (1980) *An Ordinary Life: Comprehensive locally-based residential services for mentally handicapped people.* London: Kings Fund Centre

Kings Fund (1986) *An Ordinary Working Life.* London: Kings Fund

Rolph, S, Atkinson, D, Nind, M, and Welshman, J. (eds) (2005) *Witnesses to Change: Families, learning difficulties and history.* Kidderminster: BILD

Silent Minority DVD, available from www.concordmedia.co.uk, shows what life was like for people living in the mental handicap hospitals

Legislation, policies and reports

Department of Health (2001) *Valuing people: A new strategy for learning disability for the 21st century – a white paper.* London: Department of Health

Department of Health (2006) *Our Health, Our Care, Our Say: A new direction for community services.* London: Department of Health

Department of Health (2009) *Valuing People Now.* London: Department of Health

Mencap (2004) *Treat Me Right! Campaigning report calling for better healthcare for people with a learning disability.* London: Mencap

Mencap (2007) *Death by Indifference: Report about institutional discrimination within the NHS, and people with a learning disability getting poor healthcare.* London: Mencap

Michael, J (2008) *Healthcare for All: Report of the independent inquiry into access to healthcare for people with learning disabilities.* London: Department of Health

UK Parliament (2008) *A Life Like Any Other? Human rights of adults with learning disabilities.* London: Joint Parliamentary Committee on Human Rights

Poor Law Act 1601
Lunacy Act 1845
Idiots Act 1886
Royal Commission on the Care and Control of the Feeble Minded 1908
Mental Deficiency Act 1913
Elementary Education Act 1913

NHS Act 1948

Education Act 1944

Royal Commission on Mental Health 1957

Mental Health Act 1959

Education Act 1970

Better Services for the Mentally Handicapped 1971

Education Act 1981

Mental Health Act 1983

NHS Community Care Act 1991

Disability Discrimination Act 1995

Details of more recent legislation can be found in Chapter 6

Websites

BASE British Association of Supported Employment www.base-uk.org

Easy Health www.easyhealth.org.uk

Housing Options www.housingoptions.org.uk

The Open University learning disability history research group
www.open.ac.uk/hsc/ldsite/

Unlocking the Past, the Royal Albert Hospital archive
www.unlockingthepast.org.uk

Chapter 3

Understanding how views and attitudes impact on the lives of people and their family carers

I don't like having a label, but I don't really know what term could be used instead. I feel having a label of 'learning disability' has stopped me having the opportunity to get married.

Janet

Our first experience of a manager in the small group home my son moved to was fantastic. The atmosphere of the flat was welcoming and positive. She was genuinely pleased to meet Scott and us, his parents. She really listened to Scott and almost immediately they were having a great conversation about Scott's favourite bands. She had a genuine regard for me as his mum and truly wanted to hear my views and took them on board. Imagine our disappointment when this manager left only to be replaced by someone who was just the opposite – defensive and suspicious. We no longer felt welcome in our son's home; we found it difficult to discuss things that were important to us and our son. It felt very disempowering. When Scott became very unhappy we decided it was time for him to move on. A lesson in how one person's attitude can make all the difference.

Parent of Scott, a young man with learning disabilities and autism (*taken from* Partnership Working with Family Carers of People with a Learning Disability and People with Autism, *Cowen and Hanson, 2012*)

Introduction

Already in this book you have seen how people with a learning disability have not always been treated equally or been included in family and community activities. The two quotes above also show how family carers and people with a learning disability are affected by the attitudes and behaviour of others. Even today some people with a learning disability experience negative attitudes from others. Some family carers also tell us that they face negative approaches from people that they know and also from professionals. People's negative attitudes often show themselves in unhelpful and discriminatory behaviour. Discrimination is when a person receives less favourable treatment because of their age, disability, race, religion or belief, gender or sexual orientation. Discrimination against people with a learning disability takes many forms from name calling, to denying people access to services, hostility and even violence.

This chapter looks at how attitudes toward people with a learning disability are changing, and the steps that ordinary citizens as well as paid workers can take to promote positive attitudes. The chapter also explores how different organisations have contributed to changing attitudes to people with a learning disability and their families.

Learning outcomes

This chapter will help you to:

- understand how attitudes are changing in relation to individuals with learning disabilities;

- explain some the of positive and negative aspects of being labelled as having a learning disability;

- understand the steps that can be taken to promote positive attitudes towards individuals with learning disabilities and their family carers;

- explain the role of external agencies and others in changing attitudes, policy and practice.

This chapter covers:

Level 2 LD 201 – Understand the context of supporting individuals with learning disabilities: Learning Outcome 5

How attitudes are changing in relation to individuals with learning disabilities

For all of us the attitudes and behaviour of other people towards us can have a big effect on our self esteem and confidence. The attitudes of others towards a person with a learning disability can affect how they feel about themselves and their lives, their ambitions and whether they receive equal treatment from services. Negative attitudes from others can lead to feelings of low self-esteem, low self-confidence, lack of ambition and isolation. They can restrict a person's life experiences, allowing them only limited independence and few opportunities to take risks. Alternatively positive attitudes from others can mean that a person can feel really good about who they are, proud of all they do and proud to say they have a learning disability.

How we as individuals develop our attitudes towards disabled people is the result of a complex mix of influences including the views of our close family and friends, our education, work experience and the media. Many of our current views are as a result of historical ideas about disabled people and it is only slowly that people are adopting more positive attitudes to people with a learning disability and their families.

Your family, early years experiences and your friends – the values that you were taught as a child from your close family and school are important even in adult life. Also the ideas and views that you picked up as a young adult from friends and your current friends and acquaintances.

The communities you belong to – what do the people you spend your free time with think about people with disabilities and people with learning disabilities? If you have strongly held political or religious views, how are these affecting your views of people with a learning disability?

Your work situation – as a new learning disability worker you are likely to be strongly influenced by the values and behaviour of your manager and co-workers as well as those of the family carers and friends of the people you support.

The wider cultural, social values and attitudes – how do the films and television programmes you watch show people with a learning disability? What about the newspapers and magazines that you read or the websites you visit?

Factors that influence your values and attitudes towards people with a learning disability.

Negative attitudes that can lead to negative experiences and discrimination mean that people with a learning disability face difficulties in a number of areas, such as:

- accessing public services, for example health services, education and leisure facilities, because they fail to make reasonable adjustments to meet their needs;

- feeling safe when they are out in the community and confident that the law will help and protect them;

- being recognised and treated as equal members of society, respected members of their local community whose role is recognised and valued;

- achieving and maintaining an independent life of their own, with the right support, beyond social services;

- getting paid work;

- having friends and enjoying a full and varied social life;

- having relationships;

- having children.

However, things are changing for people with a learning disability. Most people now live in the community, not in segregated services, and they go to the same shops, GP surgery, leisure centres, pubs and places of worship as their neighbours. Many children and young adults have learnt alongside pupils with learning disabilities in school because of the policies of inclusion of disabled children in mainstream education. More people are being portrayed positively in films and on the television. Slowly society is moving away from seeing children and adults with a learning disability as different and treating them as second class members of society with no rights and segregated from mainstream life. Increasingly people with learning disabilities are seen as equal members of society with the same rights as everyone else. In the last ten years people with a learning disability, family carers and professionals have noted more opportunities being available to people, including:

- more advocacy and opportunities for people to speak up and be heard;

- people having more choice and control in their life;

- less residential care and more supported living with people having their own tenancy or mortgage;

- more person centred planning and person centred support;

- young people going on to further education, getting qualifications and some getting paid jobs;

- some people working in jobs that they enjoy, with good pay;

- some people getting married or living with a partner;

- some people having families;

- better systems in place to safeguard vulnerable people;

- better access to primary health care and hospitals;

- more easy read materials available and more attention being paid to making information accessible;

- more people being known and included in their local communities;

- people being considered more as equal citizens not as patients or service users.

Positive and negative aspects of having a diagnosis or an assessment of having a learning disability

If a person has a diagnosis or an assessment that says they have a 'learning disability' there can be both positive and negative consequences from that diagnosis.

Thinking point

What do you think some of the positive and negative consequences of having a learning disability diagnosis might be?

Did your thoughts include some of the answers below?

Positive aspects of having a diagnosis of a learning disability	Negative aspects of having a diagnosis of a learning disability
• It will help you and your family to better understand your needs • It might help others to have a better understanding of your needs • It may mean you are eligible for benefits, resources, funding for support • It might give you access to specialist help or support • You are able to relate with and get support from peers with similar experiences	• It could mean you are put together with others because you have the same diagnosis, but your needs may be very different • Services are provided for a group of people and therefore aren't person centred • You are seen only in terms of your label or diagnosis – not as an individual • You might be seen in terms of what you can't do – rather than what you can do • You are treated unfairly and not as an equal member of society

People with a learning disability have in the past been treated differently because of their label; they have been seen only in terms of that label and have been grouped together with other people with the same label. However, a group of people with Down's syndrome might have nothing at all in common with each other, just as a group of women may have nothing in common with each other just because they are women. We all know that everyone is a unique individual and in any group of people there will be some people who have some things in common and other people who have nothing at all in common. Putting people together because they have the same label is the opposite of being person centred. Being person centred means that we look at the individual and their strengths and needs and provide support tailored to their needs.

Often labels, based on a diagnosis or assessment, result in people being treated differently and they have even been a way of insulting the person. There can be some positives of having a label as it can help other people understand a person's needs and in certain situations it can mean that the

Putting people together because they have the same label is the opposite of being person centred. Being person centred means looking at the individual, their strengths and needs.

person can access the right support and resources. Janet's story at the beginning of this chapter, however, shows us how having a label can mean that people assume that people with a learning disability can't care for themselves, have close relationships or a family. Sometimes these protective attitudes have been held with the best of intentions to protect the person from harm, but this has led to many people with a learning disability being treated unfairly and having their human rights taken away from them.

Terry says:

I don't mind if people know I have a learning disability as it's nothing to be ashamed of. If they know they help me and tell me stuff as I can't read.

Promoting positive attitudes towards individuals with learning disabilities and their family carers

Everyone who knows and works with a person with a learning disability has an important role in promoting positive attitudes towards them and their family carers. Modelling good practice in the way that you work with people will show others how to treat people with a learning disability with dignity and respect. You can do this in many ways including:

- supporting the person with the same respect you would want for yourself or a member of your family;

- treating each person as an individual by offering personalised service;

- listening carefully to what the person tells you and supporting them to express their wants and needs;

Listen carefully to what the person tells you and support them to express their wants and needs.

- being open to learning about cultural differences to make sure your support is truly person centred;

- respecting the person's right to privacy;

- assisting people to develop and maintain their confidence and a positive self esteem;

- supporting the person to have the skills which will help others to build relationships with them in their communities;

- providing the appropriate level of support to allow each individual to take part in ways that they are able;

- supporting people to understand their rights and to challenge discrimination;

- working with people who lead community activities to enable them to include people with a learning disability;

- ensuring the person has the opportunities to make choices and that their choices and decisions are respected.

These ideas are taken from the Dignity in Care campaign at www.dignityincare.org.uk and the book *Equality and Inclusion for Learning Disability Workers* by Rorie Fulton and Kate Richardson in this series.

Promoting positive attitudes towards family carers is also important when you are working with people with a learning disability. You can do this by:

- engaging with family members as equal care partners;
- listening carefully to the experiences of family carers and their knowledge about good support for their family member;
- keeping them informed about the support you are providing;
- supporting the person with a learning disability to keep in touch with members of their family, as they wish, if they are living away from home.

More information about working in partnership with family carers can be found in the book *Partnership Working with Family Carers of People with a Learning Disability and People with Autism*, by Alison Cowen and Jamie Hanson.

Activity

Think about three things you could do over the next two weeks to promote positive attitudes towards people with a learning disability. Discuss your ideas with your line manager or at your next team meeting, or if it is appropriate with a person you support or a family carer.

Actions by external organisations and others to change attitudes, policy and practice

Many individuals and organisations have played their part in shaping the development of attitudes and services for people with a learning disability. These changes have taken place at local, regional and national level. This section highlights some of the organisations that have worked to make changes happen.

The disabled people's movement and organisations Since the 1970s there has been a growth in the number of disability campaign groups in the UK and overseas, led by disabled people, which cover the issues affecting all people with disabilities and sensory impairments, such as the Disability Alliance, the British Council of Disabled People and Disabled Persons International. They have worked to promote the rights of people with disabilities and more positive attitudes towards disabled people. The Equality and Human Rights Commission in the UK has a statutory remit to promote and monitor human rights; and to protect, enforce and promote equality across the nine 'protected' grounds: age, disability, gender, race, religion and belief, pregnancy and maternity, marriage and civil partnership, sexual orientation and gender reassignment. For more information go to www.equalityhumanrights.com

Advocacy organisations Advocacy organisations have been active in the UK since the late 1970s, and they have been important in helping people to understand and claim their rights. Self advocacy organisations are usually led and managed by people with a learning disability. They work to support people to speak up for themselves. Some advocacy organisations provide different types of advocacy support, such as crisis and citizen advocacy. For more information see Chapter 5.

Family carers' groups The voices of family carers are increasingly recognised as vital to understanding what support is needed, as they usually know the person with a disability best. Family carers still provide most of all the unpaid support for people with a learning disability and until recent times their valuable contribution went unrecognised. Family carer organisations often exist locally and also nationally to provide mutual support but also to lobby for a better understanding of the needs of family carers. National organisations that continue to work for change and support carers include:

- Contact a Family (CAF), at www.cafamily.org.uk
- National Family Carer Network, at www.familycarers.org.uk (this organisation supports family carers of adults with a learning disability)
- Carers UK, at www.carersuk.org
- Princess Royal Trust for Carers, at www.carers.org

Campaigning organisations There are many excellent campaigning groups in the UK which call on the government for equal rights, to ensure sufficient funding is available for people's support and for change in service provision. Many also promote good practice through the production of books, information, training materials, and websites. Some of the campaigning organisations provide support for people, others don't. Campaigning organisations include Mencap, the PMLD Network, Enable in Scotland, the Campaign for a Fair Society, CAF (Contact a Family), the Learning Disability Coalition, the North West Training and Development Team and Inclusion North. These groups keep up the pressure on the government to ensure that there is funding for the support of people with a learning disability to live fulfilled lives.

User-led organisations There is an increasing number of user-led organisations of people with disabilities, where people themselves run and direct their organisations. These include Centres for Independent Living that support people with advice and information about all things to do with everyday life, such as courses, benefits, aids and adaptations, etc. There are also a growing number of user-led organisations of people with a learning disability, such as training companies and arts organisations.

Universities and colleges Many universities and colleges are working to both research and teach students in the areas of good practice for people with a learning disability. These include the Norah Fry Research Centre at the University of Bristol, the Tizard Centre at the University of Kent and the Welsh Centre for Learning Disabilities at Cardiff University. There are also many courses across the UK teaching social workers and learning disability nurses that have promoted and supported changes in attitudes to disabled people.

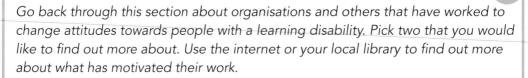

Activity

Go back through this section about organisations and others that have worked to change attitudes towards people with a learning disability. Pick two that you would like to find out more about. Use the internet or your local library to find out more about what has motivated their work.

Key points from this chapter

- People's attitudes and their behaviour towards a person with a learning disability can have a major impact on their self esteem and on what they do from day to day.

- The prejudiced attitudes that still exist towards people with a learning disability often have their origins in past negative views.

- Family carers can also experience negative attitudes because of their caring role.

- You can promote positive attitudes towards people with a learning disability by always treating them with dignity and respect and by offering person centred support.

- You show respect to family carers by engaging with them as equal partners in care.

- In the last 50 years campaigning by people with a learning disability and family carers and work by academics and others have left a positive legacy of advocacy, human rights campaigning, inclusion and person centred and community orientated services.

References and where to go for more information

References

Cowen, A and Hanson, J (2012) *Partnership Working with Family Carers of People with a Learning Disability and People with Autism.* Kidderminster: BILD

Fulton, R and Richardson, K (2011) *Equality and Inclusion for Learning Disability Workers.* Exeter: Learning Matters/BILD

Websites

Campaign for a Fair Society www.campaignforafairsociety.org

Carers UK www.carersuk.org

Contact a Family (CAF) www.cafamily.org.uk

Mencap www.mencap.org.uk

National Family Carer Network www.familycarers.org.uk (this organisation supports family carers of adults with a learning disability)

PMLD Network www.pmldnetwork.org

Princess Royal Trust for Carers www.carers.org

Valuing People www.valuingpeoplenow.dh.gov.uk

Chapter 4

Promoting communication with people with learning disabilities

Others can help me to make my own decisions and choices by discussing things with me and giving me information which is accessible. If people give me easy read information with pictures in and talk through the information with me it will make it easier for me to understand.

Jeremy

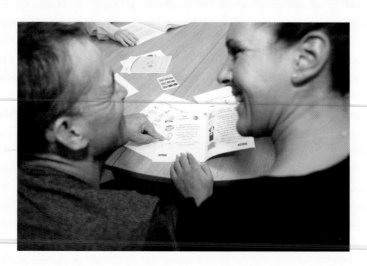

Introduction

Most of the time we take communication for granted. We express ourselves and listen to others with ease. However, people with a learning disability can often find communication challenging, both in understanding what is said to them and expressing themselves clearly. People's challenges can be in relation to understanding and expressing themselves verbally (using words) and non-verbally (not using words). Therefore it is often up to us to adjust the way we communicate so that the people with a learning disability can take the lead and be heard. When you are working in a way that respects people with a learning disability you have to make the effort to understand how they communicate and then adjust your communication to meet their needs.

Learning outcomes

This chapter will help you to:

- understand ways of adapting your verbal and non-verbal communication when communicating with a person with a learning disability;

- explain why it is important to use language that is both 'age appropriate' and 'ability appropriate' when communicating with a person with a learning disability;

- describe ways of checking whether a person has understood your communication and how to address any misunderstandings.

This chapter covers:

Level 2 LD 201 – Understand the context of supporting individuals with learning disabilities: Learning Outcome 6

Verbal and non-verbal communication

Thinking point

Think about the last two hours of your day, before you settled down to read this chapter. How many times did you communicate with other people? How did you communicate? Was this by speaking and listening, by email or text, using facial expression or signs, reading or writing?

Communication is essential for all of us for interacting and socialising with other people and making sense of the world around us. We communicate for many different reasons including:

- to express who we are;
- to express our feelings, thoughts and emotions;

- to show our preferences and make choices;
- to build relationships and make friends;
- to gain and pass on knowledge and information;
- to control our lives and develop independence.

For many people with learning disabilities, verbal and written communication can sometimes be problematic. In addition we all rely on non-verbal ways of communicating, including gesture, tone of voice and body language. We can also use signing, symbols, objects of reference and other communication aids. These are important ways to support the understanding of our communication. Often we underestimate how important non-verbal communication can be. The diagram below shows how little communication is understood through words and how much meaning is conveyed in other ways. Understanding that facial expression, body language and tone of voice carry far more meaning than the actual words we use can help us when communicating with a person with a learning disability. It means that we must look for other ways of understanding what the person is saying and ensure that we are aware of any mixed messages that our own posture or tone of voice might be giving.

How we communicate

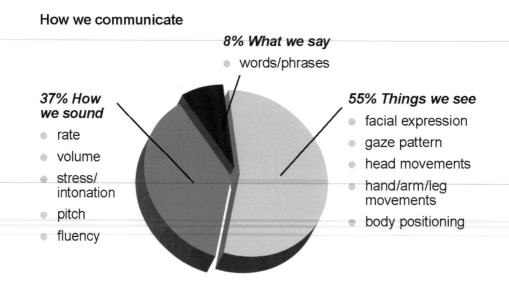

8% What we say
- words/phrases

37% How we sound
- rate
- volume
- stress/ intonation
- pitch
- fluency

55% Things we see
- facial expression
- gaze pattern
- head movements
- hand/arm/leg movements
- body positioning

Activity

Use the diagram above to help you think about a recent conversation you had with a person with a learning disability. Think about what they said, the things you could see, their facial expression, body position and gaze, and also their tone of voice. Make some short notes under the three areas of communication: what they said, the things you saw and how they sounded.

When thinking about promoting excellent communication with people with a learning disability it is important to remember the following points:

1. **Communication is a two way activity, involving understanding as well as expressing.** How much somebody is able to understand is often misjudged by other people. It is important for you to establish as far as possible how much the people you support understand, so that they can be supported to take a full part in communication.

2. **Communication is a shared activity – dependent on both 'speaker' and 'listener'.** It is not enough to focus just on the person with learning disabilities. You must also think about your own communication abilities and if necessary develop new styles and ways of interaction.

3. **Communication can be easily misunderstood.** It is easy to misunderstand what somebody is telling us – particularly if they don't use ways of communication with which you are familiar. You will need to be aware of this in your conversations and look for ways to understand.

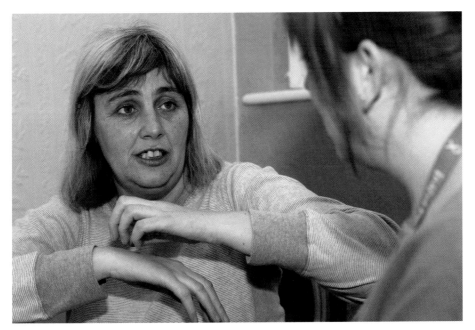

Good communication is a two way activity involving understanding as well as expressing.

Activity

Think of someone you know who has a learning disability. Can this person always make their thoughts and feelings known? What helps both you and the person with a learning disability to communicate? Have there been any times that you have not understood what they are trying to communicate with you?

Adapting your communication to aid understanding

As you try to observe and understand a person with a learning disability that you support you will start to understand the ways you might need to adapt your own communication to aid understanding.

Verbal communication: what can help?

When thinking about adapting your verbal communication it is helpful to match the types of words and sentences you use to the person's ability, understanding and experience. These questions should help you think about your verbal communication:

- Does the person understand the words you are using?
- Can the person understand the questions you ask?
- Does the person need you to shorten and simplify your sentences?

Try not to ask too many questions at once as this can be confusing and the person is likely to become quiet. It is always better to keep your language simple without being patronising. If the person doesn't seem to understand what you are trying to tell them, there are lots of things you can try – just make sure you do one at a time or you could confuse them further. If the person you are supporting doesn't understand what you are trying to say then you could try the 10 tips below.

Ten top tips for good verbal communication

1. Look at the person and give them your full attention. Remember that some people find direct eye contact difficult so get to know the person and what they feel comfortable with.

2. Use their name to attract their attention.

3. Remember to be respectful, genuine, and warm with the person.

4. Speak slowly, don't rush or carry on talking if it looks as though the person doesn't understand. Take your time and give the person time to process what you have said.

5. Be aware of the words that you use. Are you using words that the person understands and would use? Are there any cultural or gender issues you need to consider?

6. As appropriate use photos, objects or signs to supplement what you are saying to reinforce the main message and to help the person stay focused. Find out from their family or people who know them well what symbols, pictures or objects of reference the person is used to.

7. Be aware of things which may be difficult for the person to understand such as numbers, past tense or future tense, or times and dates.

8. If necessary repeat a statement or reword it in a more understandable way. To simplify what you've said use shorter sentences and fewer words.

9. Think carefully about your non-verbal communication. Avoid your body language saying something different from your words as this will be confusing.

10. Think about whether the environment is too hot, noisy or distracting or whether you need to try at a different time of day when the person is more alert. The same person may communicate differently at different times of the day or when their health is good or bad. Be sensitive to the environment and the person's needs at the time.

Non-verbal communication: what helps?

You need to be aware of your own non spoken communication as this will often be very important in helping the people you support to understand you. This will include your facial expressions, eye contact, body language and gestures as well as your tone of voice and how quickly you speak.

People who find spoken words difficult often rely on your non-verbal communication. Make sure you use it well to convey your meaning and intention. You should maximise your use of facial expression, gesture and eye contact, along with any aids such as objects or pictures to make clear what you are saying. Having an object or picture about the subject of your conversation will often help a person to remember what it is you are talking about. Always remember to think about the person with whom you are communicating. For some people the use of touch, such as a hand on their shoulder, is an important way of making contact with them. For others touch might be distressing. You must take your lead from them and what you have learnt about them from others who know them well.

Sophie and her support worker: 'I like my support workers to talk to me really nicely, friendly, lots of talking and they say, "What have you been up to?"'

Pay close attention to the other person's non spoken communication as this is a good way to understand how the person is feeling. Remember sometimes eyes and faces can communicate something different from what is being said. Everyone's non spoken communication is very individual to them. For example, usually people maintain eye contact if they want to communicate and are interested in what is happening or being discussed. Lack of eye contact can mean a person is unhappy or depressed or unwilling to communicate at that time. However, some people with autism find establishing and maintaining eye contact very difficult, so you will need to know the person well before you can truly understand their communication. Another example is body posture. People who have their legs or arms crossed usually feel withdrawn or unhappy whereas people who show an open body posture are usually more comfortable and calm. But there are cultural issues relating to body language and you need to understand the person's cultural background and history before you can really understand their body language.

Non-verbal communication differences It's not only verbal communication where there can be cultural differences. Non-verbal cues vary between cultures and can lead to misinterpretation. For example, in some Hindu communities, folding your arms is a sign of humility. In a western culture this could be a sign of stubbornness or aggression.

Lack of eye contact can be seen as a barrier to communication or even a sign of deceitfulness in some western cultures. However, Somali children are taught not to make eye contact with adults. Pictures and photographs can have different meanings in different cultures so you need to think about the cultural meaning of images that you use. It is important to spend time watching and getting to know the other person to understand their body language and tone of voice.

It is also important to be aware of what you are communicating both verbally and non-verbally and whether this is consistent. Your facial expression, the tone of your voice, how loudly you speak, the words that you use and how close you are to an individual are all very important means of communication.

You need to know that the person whom you are supporting understands the words used or what you've said. They may be unable to speak or may feel threatened by your attempts to communicate with them. In addition you may not quite understand what the person is trying to say. Unfortunately, you may think you can 'mind read' and guess what the person is thinking or trying to communicate without really knowing or understanding the person. Worse than this, you may accidentally ignore the person or fail to give them enough time.

Other things that can help the person understand include:

- using diaries or calendars;
- using 'timetables' to explain what activities people will be doing on a particular day;
- using regular events such as TV programmes –, for example, 'When we've watched *EastEnders*';
- using prompts to help the individual remember and placing these in the places that the person would see them. For example, place a photo of a bunch of keys and their mobile phone on the back of the front door to remind the person to lock up and take their keys and mobile with them. It is very important to use such objects consistently on every occasion to reinforce their understanding;
- giving information in more than one way, for example words **and** a picture.

Objects of reference can be used to represent words and ideas and are often used for people who either cannot see or understand pictures. For example, showing a person a mug to ask whether they want a drink of tea.

Pictures can be in the form of photographs, drawings or symbols. They can be added to written information to make this more accessible or understandable for people with learning disabilities. They can also be used with individuals to help them make decisions and choices, or to understand events that will happen that day. A variety of symbols and picture banks have been specially developed for use with people with learning disabilities. If these are used in the organisation you work for you should be given training in how to use them properly.

Signs are hand gestures that are used in an agreed way to communicate. Signs from British Sign Language (BSL) have been used in several vocabularies specifically for people with learning disabilities, such as Makaton and Signalong. Makaton uses signs, symbols and speech to help people with learning and/or communication difficulties to communicate. Many Makaton signs are based on BSL and are graphic, that is they show visually what the word means. For example, the sign for baby is folded arms and rocking.

Communication aids can range from simple boards or books to more sophisticated 'talking aids'. These electronic aids can be operated via eye gaze, switches, keyboards or touch screens to trigger spoken messages.

You can find more information on communication aids in the book in this series *Communicating Effectively with People with a Learning Disability* by Sue Thurman.

Lois signing to her neighbour.

Activity

Think about how you could communicate with the following people who have communication challenges. What could you do to enable and increase your and their understanding. Discuss your ideas with a colleague.

- *Shona has profound learning disabilities and cannot communicate using words. How would you check with her if she wants to go swimming after her lunch?*

- *Ranjit is deaf and uses British Sign Language. How could you explain to him that his transport home will be delayed as the minibus has broken down?*

Touch

You shouldn't automatically assume that it is appropriate to touch the person you support. Most of us allow some people to touch us and would feel uncomfortable if other people touched us or tried to touch us. This is particularly true in relation to people we do not know or do not like. In certain situations it is right to touch the person you support if it helps you to communicate with that person. Such situations might include:

- touching their arm to get their attention;

- teaching the person something 'hand-on-hand';

- 'directing' the person to a certain thing or task;

- comforting a person when they are upset.

However, as workers we need to be aware of the limits of our job role and always ask ourselves, 'Is this ok?' Don't just assume that it's ok – how might that person feel about being touched?

How to communicate in an 'age appropriate' and 'ability appropriate' way with people with learning disabilities

Age appropriate means that communication should be right for the age of the person you are communicating with. This means being person centred in your approach and showing that you uphold the values of equality, dignity and respect in the way you behave. It is important that we do not use child like language or words with adults as this undermines their age and it is condescending and patronising. You must always ensure that all communication is pitched at a level the person can understand, such as by using signs, pictorial references, large print and any other approaches to enable good communication and show our respect. Good two way communication is essential if we want people to be in control of their own lives!

Activity

Think of a time when you didn't quite understand when someone was trying to communicate a difficult idea to you. This might be a professional such as a lawyer or accountant or it might be when trying to read instructions. How did this make you feel?

At some time all of us have been in situations where we were not quite sure what was being said. It could be that the people in the meeting were using 'jargon', professional language that only means something to the people in that line of work, such as in the legal profession. Use of jargon can make people feel not as 'good' or as intelligent as others and can prevent the understanding of what is being communicated.

Communicating in age appropriate ways means in ways that are right for the person's age; communicating in ability appropriate ways is about communicating in ways that are right for the person's ability. When you are communicating with people with a learning disability you need to be aware of the words you use – are they jargon, or too difficult to understand in any way because they are not part of everyday conversation? If the words are difficult then you need to think about using words that are easier to understand for the person and their ability. People with a learning disability are very clear about this – they say 'no jargon and no long words!'

Activity

Think about a better way of explaining these words to a person with a learning disability

Complicated words and concepts	Simpler explanation using no jargon
A review meeting	
Advocacy	
Hydrotherapy	
Staff rota	
Confidential information	

Assessment

Supported living

Tenancy agreement

Can you think of any other words that are used where you work that people with a learning disability might have difficulty in understanding? Could you use another word or phrase?

Some people with a learning disability have a communication passport that they carry with them to help others communicate with them effectively. The passport explains to new friends and workers how best to communicate with them. For people with complex communication needs a communications chart might also be used. A chart like the one below helps people who don't know the person very well or who are new to supporting them. It is one of the person centred thinking tools.

At this time/ when this is happening	When the person does this	We think it means	And we should
When Mary is at home	Mary shakes her purse and says 'me!'	She wants to walk to the local newsagent and choose something to buy	Mary needs support to go, and a reminder to wear a coat if cold. She can buy whatever she wants, usually this is a TV magazine and a chocolate bar. She pays for them herself and the shop keeper is very friendly.

With thanks to Helen Sanderson Associates

Ways to check whether a communication has been understood and how to address misunderstandings

Communication breakdowns can happen for a wide variety of reasons. Sometimes what a person says and what they mean can be different; sometimes the words we use are ambiguous or too complex; occasionally we misunderstand a person's non-verbal signals. Even if you are an excellent communicator and have a great understanding of the communication needs of the person you work with, there will be occasions when communication breaks down. Being prepared for this and having some strategies to repair the situation is important for learning disability workers.

There are a number of things you can do to check whether a person with a learning disability has understood a recent communication between you. You can also use these ideas to check whether you have understood their communication with you.

- Ask the person to repeat what has been said back to you.

- You could repeat their communication with you back to them and ask, 'Have I got it right?'

- If you are seeking to understand a person's non-verbal communication you can check your understanding with other people who know the person well. For example, does Mandeep smile to attract attention when she is bored as well as to show she is enjoying an activity?

- Ensure that you never make any assumptions.

If you don't understand what someone is trying to tell you, or they do not understand what you are trying to say to them – don't panic! It is never a good idea to just pretend that you understand. If you ask them to repeat their communication, make sure that you apologise for not understanding and never blame them for not communicating clearly. You could say something like, 'I'm sorry, I didn't understand what you said. Please can you say it again?' Or you could ask them, 'Show me.' You could also ask a colleague or one of their family or friends who might know the person better to help you understand.

You could also use pictures or signs – the person may be able to point or sign more easily than speaking. Take your time and be creative. Give the person time to express themselves in other ways.

People themselves can also be very creative in helping others to understand them, such as fetching other people, drawing pictures, acting events out or using other ways.

Key points from this chapter

- We all have a right to communicate and to communication support.
- Communication is a basic human right that most of us take for granted. Almost everyone can communicate but not all people can communicate in the same way as us. Things that can help are:
  - positive body language;
  - smiling (if suitable);
  - nodding;
  - moving towards the person;
  - showing you are interested.
- Find out about the communication preferences of the person you support.
- You can used shared activities, listening to the person, observation and waiting for the person to communicate as ways of finding out about how a person communicates.
- Communicate in a way that is right for the person's age; do not use childlike language or words as it can be condescending and patronising.
- Get to know the person you are communicating with well so that you can find the best way to communicate verbally and non-verbally with them.

References and where to go for more information

References

Goldbart, J and Caton, S (2010) *Communication and People with the Most Complex Needs: What works and why it is essential.* London: Mencap

~~**Grove, N (2000)** *See What I Mean.* Kidderminster: BILD~~

Mencap (2008) *Your Guide to Communicating with People with a Learning Disability.* London: Mencap

Thurman, S (2011) *Communicating Effectively with People with a Learning Disability.* Exeter: Learning Matters/BILD

Thurman, S (2009) *BILD Guide: Communication is a human right.* Kidderminster: BILD

Websites

Communication Matters www.communicationmatters.org.uk (for information on augmentative and alternative communication)

Gloucestershire Total Communication www.totalcommunication.org.uk (for information and links to all types of alternative communication)

Inclusive Technology www.inclusive.co.uk

Sense – UK Deafblind Charity (and associated disabilities) www.sense.org.uk

Chapter 5

Understanding the principles of advocacy, empowerment and active participation

Jim (not his real name) lives in a large residential home for people with learning disabilities. He is completely dependent on others for personal care as he is physically disabled and uses a wheelchair. Just Advocacy became involved in the home when there were concerns about the quality of care.

Jim made himself known to our advocate. He had lots to say about his life in the home and about what he wanted for himself; no-one had listened before. Jim's relationship with our advocate was very important to him, but he was frightened about saying what troubled him to those looking after him in case it made things worse for him. He trusted the advocate to keep things confidential until he was ready to speak out.

Jim had lived in the home for over 20 years, since he was a child. He had few experiences outside the home, but knew that he wanted to move. With our advocate's help others began to see Jim as a real person, with a personality, feelings and wishes of his own. We hope that he will be moving to a place of his choice before long.

Jim's story is taken from www.justadvocacy.org.uk

Fahmida was referred because she had moved into respite care when her mother became too ill to care for her and it had become necessary to find somewhere permanent for her to live. Fahmida has high support needs and can use limited words to communicate, although this tends to be repetitive and she will mostly answer 'Yes' to questions. The advocate met Fahmida regularly to establish her method of communication and after a while it became apparent that Fahmida lacked the capacity to make an informed decision about where she wanted to live. The advocate attended all meetings where decisions were being made about Fahmida's future and used the 'Watching Brief' to ask professionals questions about why they were proposing a particular course of action. During the time the advocate had spent with Fahmida it became clear that being able to access a garden and to watch the birds from her window, although seemingly very small issues, were important to her. Fahmida also liked to be able to access the shops, particularly to buy chocolate buttons! The advocate was able to ensure that others knew these matters were of significant importance to Fahmida.

The advocate went with Fahmida to visit her proposed new accommodation and took photographs which were put into a large book to use as prompts for the advocate and carers to talk about her new home. The advocate made many visits with Fahmida to the new home together and was able to identify that Fahmida was very relaxed there and accessed the garden each time.

Fahmida's story is taken from www.advocacyresource.org.uk

Introduction

As you saw in Chapter 2 on the history of the lives of people with a learning disability, over the years people with learning disabilities have been treated differently from people without a learning disability. Many people with a learning disability have not had the same opportunities as other citizens in terms of an education, work, healthcare, housing and a family life. People with a learning disability have felt that their voices have not been heard and they have been excluded and discriminated against.

In the last hundred years many people who have also experienced exclusion and discrimination have come together in groups and to form movements demanding equality and their human rights. These have included the women's suffrage movement seeking votes for women, the black civil rights and the gay pride movements and the disability rights movement. Some consider that one of the last social movements in the UK is that of people with a learning disability. From the late 1980s there has been ongoing lobbying by people with a learning disability and their allies for their greater participation and empowerment and a full acknowledgement of their human rights. There has been a steady growth of people with a learning disability speaking up and having a voice. The self-advocacy movement has played a major part in this.

Learning outcomes

This chapter will help you to:

- explain the term 'social inclusion';
- understand the meaning of the term 'advocacy';
- describe different types of advocacy;
- describe ways to build empowerment and active participation into everyday support of people with a learning disability.

This chapter covers:

Level 2 LD 201 – Understand the context of supporting individuals with learning disabilities: Learning Outcome 4

What is social inclusion?

Social inclusion means being included and playing a meaningful part in the life of your community, being a valued and respected member of society.

Thinking point

Think of a time when you have felt excluded from something. How did it make you feel? Were you able to change the situation or did you need support to do this?

For people with a learning disability social inclusion means taking part in social activities, having relationships and being respected by other people. It means being able to do the same things everyone else does. People with a learning disability tell us that inclusion means two important things: interacting with others, particularly friends, family and people in their community; and also accessing community facilities and taking part in community activities.

Social inclusion is a way of involving individuals or groups of people with a learning disability, who might not have had the same life chances as other members of society because of their learning disability. Social inclusion is about making sure that people with learning disabilities are fully involved in all aspects of their own lives, and have the same chances as other members of society to be involved in activities and services.

Social inclusion is a key principle in *Valuing People Now* (2009), the government policy for services for people with a learning disability in England. It says, 'Inclusion means being able to participate in all the aspects of community – to work, learn, get about and meet people, be part of social networks, and access goods and services – and to have the support to do so'. *Valuing People Now* also acknowledges that not all people with a learning disability are empowered to become active citizens. It says the policy and our society need to be inclusive of all groups, taking particular account of those who are generally more excluded, including:

- people with more complex needs;
- people from black and minority ethnic groups and newly arrived communities;
- people with a learning disability and an autistic spectrum condition;
- people with learning disabilities who are offenders in custody and the community.

Unfortunately in reality many people with learning disabilities still face social isolation, use segregated services, and are discriminated against by public services and only 7% of people of working age are in employment. Whether you provide a service to people with a learning disability or you work providing direct support you can contribute to the social inclusion of people with a learning disability.

Here are some practical ideas about how to promote the social inclusion of people with a learning disability that you know or support:

- Make time to talk to the person you support about things they are interested in and enjoy, rather than just focusing on their care needs.

- Support the person to find out about and visit local community facilities where they can meet people and take part in activities such as a local pub, social or sports club, place of worship, etc.

- Support the person to visit or stay in touch with their family and friends through visits, or by phone, text or email.

- Support the person to use local services such as shops or transport, or to go out in their local area more, making sure they have the right support to do this.

- Find out about local opportunities for volunteering, work placements or paid work and how they could access them.

- Talk about social inclusion issues with colleagues or in team meetings or supervision.

Activity

Discuss with a person you support, or a work colleague or the family carer of a person you support, one way that you could promote inclusion in your work.

Thinking point

Think about a typical day in your own life. What kind of things do you do?

Then think about a typical day in the life of a person with a learning disability. What might they do?

Your day may include...	A person with a learning disability's life may include...
Going to work	Going to a day centre
Going shopping	Going to an event, such as a disco for people with a learning disability
Meeting up with friends in the pub, going to a concert or to a restaurant	Spending time with other people with a learning disability/members of staff
Spending time with your partner	

Things are changing and many people with learning disabilities have lives like everyone else. They have jobs, hobbies, friends and partners. However, many people with learning disabilities still lead lives that are 'different', often only spending time with other people with a learning disability or members of staff, not having the opportunity to try new hobbies or experiences or spend time with new people.

Our job is to support people with learning disabilities to be included and become equal members within society. You can find out more about social inclusion and also diversity, equality and discrimination in the book *Equality and Inclusion for Learning Disability Workers* by Rorie Fulton and Kate Richardson in this series.

What is advocacy?

Advocacy means to support a person to speak up for themselves, get their wishes and ideas heard and acted on. Most of us at some time in our lives speak up for someone else, or hope that someone will speak up for us. Advocacy is a way for people with learning disabilities to be heard and to promote their human rights.

An advocate is usually an independent person who can support a person with a learning disability to have their voice heard, and who can also support them to make informed choices. The advocate gets to know the person, their wishes and needs, and then represents them in situations when others are making decisions about their support. The advocate's role is to make sure that the person's views, feelings, wishes and rights are being listened to and valued. The advocate is independent from services and families so only has what is best for the person in mind. In some cases the advocate will make sure that those people making decisions for a person who lacks capacity do what is best for the person and not just what is best for other people who are involved with that person.

The role of an advocate will vary according to the needs of the person they are working with, but an advocate can support a person:

- to find out information and make sure the person understands it, which could mean making information accessible;
- during a complaints process;

- to find and visit a person to give them professional advice;

- to go to meetings and communicate their ideas clearly;

- to weigh up a range of options and make decisions;

- when necessary to promote a person's rights and interests when they are not able to say what they want to happen.

An advocate is a good listener and supports a person to get their ideas and wishes heard.

An advocate is someone who is a good listener and good at communicating with different people and in different ways. They help people with a learning disability who:

- may want support to make changes in their lives;

- find it hard to speak at meetings;

- need help to find information and understand what their choices are;

- want to get to know more people and be more involved in their community.

Advocacy is a way of supporting the human rights of people with learning disabilities; it is a way to give people with learning disabilities more choice and control over their own lives by finding out the options available to them.

Different types of advocacy

There are several different types of advocacy, which we will look at in detail below.

Independent professional advocacy

This is advocacy from a professional expert such as a lawyer or a paid advocate who is commissioned to speak up on behalf of an individual or a group in a professional capacity, for example, in a court or during a review meeting. They may or may not be paid for doing this.

Self advocacy

This is when people speak up for themselves and through organised groups. Some of these are known as people first groups.

People First, a self advocacy organisation, set up and run by people with learning difficulties (disabilities) say:

Self advocacy is people with learning difficulties speaking up for ourselves. Self advocacy is important because many people with learning difficulties spend their lives being told what to do. If you are always told what to do and never listened to you can get to the point where you don't even know how to make a decision for yourself. Speaking up is something people with learning difficulties need support to learn to do and other people need to learn how to understand us.

Self advocacy has taken forward the idea that people with learning difficulties need to be listened to. Professionals and carers who run services for people with learning difficulties should ask us what we want because no one knows better than us ourselves.

To find out more about People First go to www.peoplefirstltd.com

Group or self advocacy

People First go on to say:

Self advocacy groups are for people with learning difficulties to meet and:

- share their experiences;
- support each other;
- learn to speak up;
- find out about their rights;
- speak up to local services about what is important to them.

There are local self advocacy groups all across the country but groups are all different and some have problems getting financial support.

People First believe that more money should be put into self advocacy. Self advocacy can change lives and all people with learning difficulties should have access to it.

People First also believe that 'self advocacy groups need to be user led, which means they should be fully run and controlled by people with learning difficulties ourselves. This way self advocacy groups are doing exactly what we tell other services to do – give us the same chances as everyone else to have responsibility and jobs to be treated with respect'.

You can find out about self advocacy organisations in your area if you live in England and Wales from the database on this website: www.actionforadvocacy.org.uk

If you live in Scotland you can find an advocacy group on the Scotland Independent Advocacy Alliance website at www.siaa.org.uk. In Northern Ireland ask your local council about independent advocacy in your area.

Peer advocacy

Peer advocacy is when a person with a learning disability supports another person with a learning disability to speak up for themselves. Sometimes it might be because the person being supported may have problems communicating or they may lack the confidence to speak up for themselves, so their peer advocate can support them.

Issue based advocacy

Issue based advocacy is often used when a person has a big decision to make and they need support to understand the choices available to them and what rights they have. This may be a decision about moving home, going away to college or deciding on a particular course of treatment recommended by a doctor. The advocate is there to support the person with their choices; they always take the person's side and support them even if other people such as family members and professionals want them to make a different choice.

Citizen advocacy

A citizen advocate is a member of the public who volunteers to support someone to speak up for themselves.

Citizen advocacy involves the creation of long-term partnerships between two people. In each partnership, one of the partners:

- helps the other to safeguard their human rights;
- provides the other with moral support;
- gives some practical help.

John O'Brien defines citizen advocacy in this way: 'An ordinary citizen develops a relationship with another person who risks social exclusion or other unfair treatment because of a disability. As the relationship develops, the advocate chooses ways to understand, respond to and represent the other person's interests as if they were the advocate's own.'

Citizen advocacy is:

- independent of services received by the person with a disability and their family;
- a partnership in which the advocate's sole loyalty is to their partner;
- not a service to the person with a disability, but a resource for them within a relationship freely entered into;
- directed by the two people in the partnership.

Taken from www.dunfermlineadvocacy.org

Keith

Keith has a job volunteering in a local charity shop. He didn't require support whilst he was working there, but staff walked with Keith to work and then met him when he'd finished. Keith told his advocate that he wanted to become more independent and walk to work by himself. His advocate respected him and listened to his wishes. His staff realised how important this was for Keith. They then reflected about the best way to support Keith to achieve his goal and advocated on his behalf with everyone in Keith's circle of support to develop a 'walk to work' plan, that Keith felt comfortable and safe with.

It has been a gradual process – eight months so far. After crossing the main roads, staff would leave Keith to continue part of the journey alone. This distance grew further as Keith developed his knowledge of the route and his confidence grew. They kept checking with Keith that he was happy with his progress and there were lots of points to celebrate. Keith can now walk all the way to work, after he is supported to cross the main roads. He is so proud of his achievement and the independence he's gained. The next stage is to look at crossing roads and to support Keith to become fully independent.

Keith is supported by an advocate

With thanks to MacIntyre for this story

Independent Mental Capacity Advocate (in England and Wales)

In England and Wales the Mental Capacity Act (2005) sets out when and how decisions can be made for people who may lack capacity to make a particular decision at a certain time. If a person with a learning disability has been deemed to lack capacity to make a particular decision for themselves and if they have no family or friends who can make a 'best interest decision' then an Independent Mental Capacity Advocate (IMCA) can be used. An IMCA can be used to help support decisions about medical treatment and changes in accommodation.

You can find out more about the Mental Capacity Act (2005) and Independent Mental Capacity Advocates from www.dh.gov.uk and from SCIE at www.scie.org.uk

In Scotland, the Adults with Incapacity Act (Scotland) 2000 provides a similar framework to safeguard the welfare and support of people who lack capacity due to a mental disorder or inability to communicate. In Northern Ireland there is currently no legislation covering advocacy for people who lack capacity.

If you work in an organisation that provides support or a service to people with a learning disability and you think a person you know might benefit from independent advocacy then you can find out about local advocacy services in Scotland, Wales and England at www.siaa.org.uk and www.actionforadvocacy.org.uk.

Building empowerment and active participation into day to day support

Building empowerment

Empowerment is about having or taking more control over all aspects of your life. As you learnt in Chapter 2, in the past many people with a learning disability had very little power over decisions that affected them. For the people who lived in the old long stay hospitals life was institutionalised and decisions about daily activities, food, clothing and work were taken for people by the professionals who managed the hospital. People were disempowered by an authoritarian regime. Even today some services are still run in a similar way to the old hospitals and the people they support have little control over many aspects of their life.

You cannot give another person choice and control over their life, you cannot give them empowerment, instead you can give them the confidence, skills and knowledge to lead their own lives. The best way to support people with learning disabilities to combat exclusion and discrimination in their lives is by helping them to become empowered. This means helping them to:

- know their rights;
- develop their self-confidence;
- gain the self-belief to address discrimination.

You can empower a person in many ways, such as:

- supporting them to make choices and decisions in their daily life by making sure they have all the information they need in a way that they can understand;

- supporting them to access a local independent advocacy group or have an advocate;

- helping them to know about their rights and to speak up if they think their rights have been breached;

- helping them to access and use complaints processes if they feel they have received a poor service;

- ensuring they have a person centred plan which is regularly updated and communicated to everyone who supports them;

- ensuring they have the opportunities to be part of their local community or pursue hobbies and interests and live a fulfilled life.

Working in a person centred way is an important ingredient in supporting people to become more empowered. It means making sure that the person with learning disabilities is at the centre of everything that happens and that they are involved in all of the choices that affect their life.

Most people faced with important or difficult decisions feel worried that they are making the right decision or just feel so concerned that they can't make a decision at all. Decision making is a skill and it takes practice for us to feel confident with our decisions – and even then there are times when we feel we haven't made the right one.

The things that help us make decisions are having enough information, given to us in a way that we can understand to help us know what the decision is, and knowing what the consequences are of choosing one way or another. People with learning disabilities can find it more difficult to make decisions for themselves as they may not understand the decision and the options that there are. This is why it is important that we support people with learning disabilities by giving them information in a way that they can understand. Supporting people with making their own choices is one way in which we can empower them to become independent.

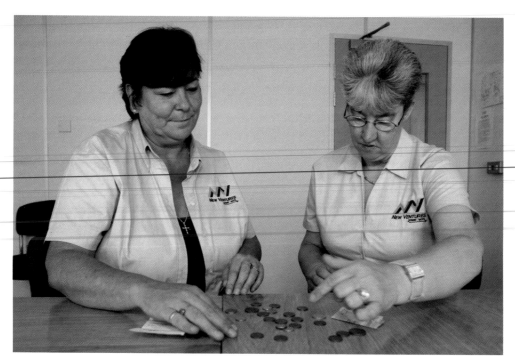

Supporting a person to develop their skills is one aspect of empowerment.

Janet says:

I am confident about making everyday choices for myself and need some support with money, letters such as bills, and more difficult decisions such as operations.

I like to have information to help me make choices. I like people to talk through what the options are, what is going to happen, etc. and I like them to explain written information so that I understand what this might mean.

I have a key worker who is supporting me to develop my skills around literacy and numeracy. My key worker does this in a practical way like using coins to count out money. I go to Morrison's to buy bread with support from staff, just in case I get 'stuck' then the staff can help me and I find this really useful.

Active participation

Active participation is a way of working that recognises an individual's right to participate in the activities and relationships of everyday life as independently as possible; the individual is regarded as an active partner in their own care or support, rather than a passive recipient of care.

In the past the traditional model of services for people with learning disabilities was to 'care' for people, and staff were known as care workers or care assistants. This meant the general approach was to 'do things for people' especially for people who had few independent living skills. So care assistants would typically cook the tea, make the drinks and clean, and people would sit in the lounge with nothing to do except watch TV. This has been called the 'hotel model' of support.

The current model of support is very different from this 'hotel model' of support for people with learning disabilities. Now the role of the support worker is to enable and support independence by involving people in day to day activities such as making the bed, shopping or gardening. Sometimes we refer to people being actively engaged, this means people are spending their time in an active and involved way rather than as an observer or having no fulfilling activities to do.

The role of the support worker is to enable and support independence by involving people in day to day activities.

> *Val*
>
> Being sensitive to small details is so important.
>
> Having a bath is a real part of Val's routine. She has a bath each morning and sometimes asks staff for another bath in the evening. She is often supported to have a couple of baths a day, and doing this enables Val to be in control of her life and to do the things that matter to her. She doesn't have a long soak, just a quick bath, so it would have been easy for staff to assume this routine wasn't very important, but they were sensitive to realise that just because she rushes through an activity doesn't mean it's not important to her.
>
> *With thanks to MacIntyre for this story*

There is more information about active participation in the book *Person Centred Approaches When Supporting People with a Learning Disability* by Liz Tilly in this series.

How does active participation benefit a person?

When people are supported to actively participate in all aspects of their lives, then over time they will gain more skills, become more independent and need less staff support, and so they increase in confidence and self-esteem.

People with learning disabilities need more than a person centred plan; they need support from people that enables them to achieve it. Active participation enables people to participate successfully in meaningful activities and relationships. Active support benefits the person because:

- it promotes mental and physical health and personal development;
- it helps them keep fit and mentally alert;
- it gives a sense of personal worth;
- it allows the person to express who they are;
- it establishes the person's common interests with other people;
- it develops their talents and allows them to show what they can do;
- it demonstrates independence and autonomy;
- it enables them to look after themselves and their daily needs;
- it provides for the basis of friendships and living together.

Taken from *Person Centred Active Support* (Mansell, Brown et al. 2005)

References and where to go for more information

References

Fulton, R and Richardson, K (2011) *Equality and Inclusion for Learning Disability Workers*. Exeter: Learning Matters and BILD

Hardie, E and Brooks, L (2009) *Brief Guide to the Mental Capacity Act*. Kidderminster: BILD

Mansell, J et al. (2005) *Person Centred Active Support: A handbook*. Brighton: Pavilion

Tilly, L (2011) *Person Centred Approaches When Supporting People with a Learning Disability*. Exeter: Learning Matters and BILD

Legislation, policies and reports

The Mental Capacity Act (2005) is used in England and Wales.

In Scotland, the Adults with Incapacity (Scotland) Act 2000 applies – further information can be found on www.scotland.gov.uk

Northern Ireland currently has no specific legislation around mental capacity.

Department of Health (2009) *Valuing People Now*. London: Department of Health

Websites

Action for Advocacy www.actionforadvocacy.org.uk

Mencap www.mencap.org.uk

SCIE www.scie.org.uk

Scottish Independent Advocacy Alliance www.siaa.org.uk

Valuing People www.valuingpeoplenow.dh.gov.uk (*England and Wales*)

Chapter 6

Understanding the legislation and policies that support the human rights and inclusion of people with learning disabilities

The Welsh Assembly government believes that it is important that everyone is able to play a full part in a modern society. Perhaps more than any other group, people with a learning disability are vulnerable to social exclusion and discrimination. Therefore, barriers should be removed that prevent them assuming their equal place in society.

Statement on Policy & Practice for Adults with a Learning Disability (Wales 2007)

We recognise that services could do more to help people with learning disabilities to achieve a full life. Our main aim is to help them to be included – in community life, in education, in leisure and recreation, in day opportunities and particularly in employment...To achieve these goals means considerable change... At the centre of this is a major shift to person centred and needs-led approaches, which put the individual at the heart of any decisions made.

Same as You? A review of services for people with learning disabilities (Scottish Executive 2000)

People with a learning disability in Northern Ireland do not enjoy equality of opportunity and are often excluded from the opportunities that other citizens enjoy... there is evidence of progress having been made, but in order to fully tackle these difficulties there is a need for major co-ordinated developments in support and services and a continuing change in attitudes over at least the next 15 years... *The Equal Lives Review* is based on 5 core values... Citizenship, social inclusion, empowerment, working together and individual support.

Equal Lives: Review of policy and services for people with a learning disability in Northern Ireland (2005)

The starting point for the new strategy is the reaffirmation of the four guiding principles set out in Valuing People... rights, independent living, control and inclusion.

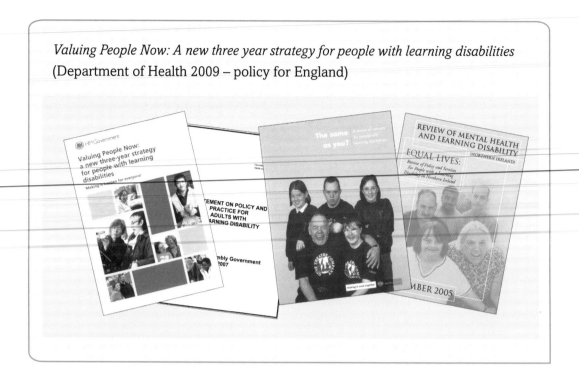

Valuing People Now: A new three year strategy for people with learning disabilities
(Department of Health 2009 – policy for England)

Introduction

Many workers don't have time to consider the legal and policy framework that affects their day to day work. Often people say they are too busy getting on with the job, but you need to know about the legal framework because a range of laws impact on what you do. These can relate to issues such as health and safety, data protection, human rights, consent to treatment, and the list goes on. Laws are often put in place to protect people and organisations. This will include the people you support, their families and friends and also you and your colleagues as employees. When you are supporting a person with a learning disability you need to know about the legal framework as you have a duty to ensure you don't breach any legislation. In addition, each country in the UK has produced a strategy or plan to promote the rights of people with learning disabilities to be included within society, and to enjoy the same opportunities and life chances as everyone else. They set out how support should be delivered to enable people to live as full citizens. The laws and national policies therefore provide a framework for what you do and can guide how you support people.

The main UK learning disability strategy or policy documents

Name of document	Published by	Country
Valuing People and Valuing People Now	Department of Health 2001 and 2009 from www.dh.gov.uk	England
Same as You? A review of services for people with learning disabilities	Scottish Executive 2000 from www.scotland.gov.uk	Scotland
Equal Lives: Review of policy and services for people with a learning disability in Northern Ireland	Department of Health and Social Services and Public Safety 2005 from www.dhsspsni.gov.uk	Northern Ireland
The Statement on Policy and Practice for Adults with a Learning Disability	Report to the National Assembly for Wales 2007 www.wales.gov.uk	Wales

Activity

Find out more about the relevant policy on support for people with a learning disability, for the country you work in. Ask your colleagues and manager how your organisation is working to implement the policy.

***Fulfilling the Promises* (2001)** This learning disability policy for Wales stressed that people with learning disabilities have the same value and status as everyone else and have an equal right to expect:

- good education;
- good health;
- good housing;
- safety and financial security;
- protection from harm;
- positive roles in the community and in the family;
- opportunities to find work;
- opportunities to learn and improve their skills;
- civic rights.

The ***Statement on Policy and Practice for Adults with a Learning Disability (Wales 2007)*** is the most recent policy document for Wales that repeats the commitment to the three key principles of policy and practice: equal rights and full citizenship; support to lead an ordinary life; and for people to be treated as individuals. The policy covers the key areas of advocacy, person centred planning, transition, day opportunities, employment, accommodation and independence.

***Valuing People* (2001)** and ***Valuing People Now* (2009)** have similar themes to *Fulfilling the Promises*, outlining the strategy for people with learning disabilities in England, to help make sure that they and their families have the same opportunities and life chances as other people. The strategy documents also deal with the areas of employment, housing, families, health, workforce issues and advocacy, amongst others.

Valuing People was the first Government White Paper, for England, about people with a learning disability for 30 years, since the White Paper *Better Services for the Mentally Handicapped* was produced in 1971.

Thinking point

Think about some of the things that you take for granted, such as having the right to express your opinions and expecting them to be heard; through to more practical issues of getting a job, or accessing health services. Then imagine what it might be like if you were denied these opportunities.

What does this mean for the person with a learning disability?

All of the pieces of national policy and guidance highlighted above underpin everything that we do when we work with people who have a learning disability. On a day-to-day basis these policies mean that organisations now have plans in place to make sure that people with learning disabilities have independent and 'ordinary lives', doing the kinds of things that other members of society do, such as having a good education, a home and a job. The person with learning disabilities can expect to be treated as an equal member of society.

Legislation and policies that promote human rights, inclusion and citizenship of people with a learning disability

There are three main pieces of legislation you need to know about in your role as a learning disability worker:

- the Human Rights Act 1998;
- the Mental Capacity Act 2005 (England and Wales) or the Adults with Incapacity (Scotland) Act 2000;
- the Equality Act 2010.

You will also need to know about the policies and procedures of your organisation, which should reflect the legislation. If you work as a personal assistant directly employed by a person with learning disabilities and/or their family carers there may not be the policies and procedures that you would

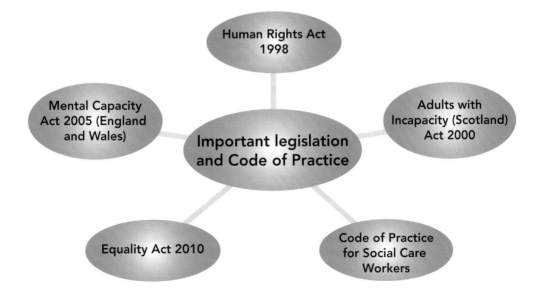

find in an organisation. Your contract of employment and the agreed ways of working that your employer discusses with you will form the basis of how you should work. Whatever your work you need to know about these key laws on equality, rights and inclusion and you must work within the law at all times.

The Human Rights Act 1998

One of the most important laws for you to get to know and understand is the Human Rights Act 1998. Human rights are based on the following core values:

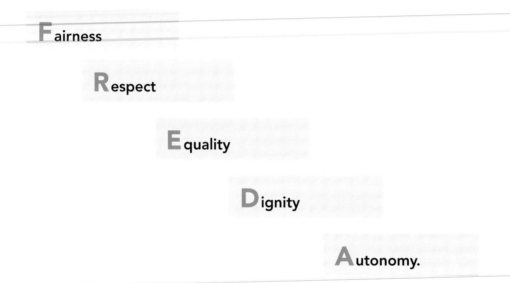

Fairness

Respect

Equality

Dignity

Autonomy.

Activity

Discuss the FREDA values at your next supervision or team meeting. Ask your colleagues how your organisation promotes these values.

These are often called the FREDA values. The Human Rights Act requires public authorities in the UK – including the government, hospitals and social services – to treat people with fairness, equality, dignity and respect. So the Act provides a legal framework within which service providers must operate, and at the same time a legal framework within which individuals can demand to be treated with respect. In this way, the Human Rights Act provides each of us with a powerful means of protection against discrimination and injustice. The Act is especially important for people with learning disabilities, who often need support from others to live their lives. The Human Rights Act says that all providers of public services must make sure they do not breach the human rights of people with learning disabilities. Here, providers of public services include staff in residential homes and day services as well as workers who support people in their own homes. An important part of your job is keeping in mind the human rights of the individual you are supporting in everything that you do. You may also need to stand up for their human rights.

All of the rights set out in the Human Rights Act belong to and apply to people with learning disabilities. The following five rights are often the most relevant:

- the right to not be tortured or treated in an inhuman or degrading way (article 3);

- the right to respect for private and family life, home and correspondence (article 8);

- the right to life (article 2);

- the right to liberty (article 5);

- the right not to be discriminated against (article 14).

The right to not be tortured or treated in an inhuman or degrading way

This right is not just or mainly about torture. The right to not be treated in an inhuman or degrading way is highly relevant to people with learning disabilities.

According to the Human Rights Act,

- inhuman treatment means treatment causing severe mental or physical harm;

- degrading treatment means treatment that is grossly humiliating and undignified.

Only the most serious kinds of mistreatment are covered by this right. Whether or not treatment is inhuman or degrading will depend on the particular circumstances of the case. When they decide if the way someone was treated was inhuman or degrading, they will think about lots of things including the person's age, sex, health status and how long this bad treatment went on for. It is important to point out that the treatment does not need to be deliberate – it is the impact it has on the person with learning disabilities that matters. For example, supporting a person to get up, washed and dressed in the morning and not taking account of their dignity and need for privacy.

Organisations, families, learning disability workers and members of the public must actively protect people with learning disabilities from inhuman or degrading treatment, whoever this is caused by. For example, if you know that someone you support is being abused you must do something about it. By not doing anything you may be breaching the person's right not to suffer this kind of treatment.

The book *Principles of Safeguarding and Protection for Learning Disability Workers* by Simon Bickerton in this series gives more information on what you must do in such a situation.

Activity

Talk to your line manager or your employer if you are a personal assistant. Find out exactly what you should do if you think a person's human rights are being breached.

The right to respect for private and family life, home and correspondence

On rare occasions, public authorities (such as social services) can restrict or limit this right. However, if they do restrict this right they need to be clear why they have done it and it must be lawful, necessary and proportionate. A proportionate restriction is one that is appropriate and not excessive. Organisations supporting people with learning disabilities need not only to respect this right but also to make sure it is respected. For example, social services may need to provide extra support to help a family headed by a person with learning disabilities to stay together.

Respect for family life

Family life does not just mean blood relatives; it also covers close and personal ties of a family kind. The right to respect for family life includes being able to live together and, in situations where this is not possible, having regular contact. This right is important for people with learning disabilities, especially if there is a risk they will be separated from their partner, children or other family members, or are at risk of having very limited contact with them. Just the idea of being separated from their parents, partner or children is enough to fill most people with dread and horror. Yet this is by no means an unusual experience for people with learning disabilities. Families that include a person with a learning disability may also face unnecessary intrusion or feel overwhelmed by their responsibilities, which can destroy family life.

A number of reasons are given for separating people with learning disabilities from their family. People with learning disabilities may be placed in residential accommodation far from home and family; this makes it difficult for them to stay in contact.

In some circumstances a local authority may have a concern about whether a person with a learning disability is able to be a good parent to their child. These are complex situations as those working with the person need to balance the rights of the parent and the rights of the child. Your job may involve supporting a person with learning disabilities to be able to stay with or near their family or to look after and bring up their own children. Remember, it is their human right to do so, and any restriction on this must be lawful, necessary and proportionate.

Respect for private life

The Human Rights Act defines 'private life' broadly. Private life is not just about privacy, it includes things such as:

- being able to live your personal life as you choose;
- being able to form relationships with others as you wish;
- being able to take part in the life of the community;
- your physical and mental wellbeing;
- having access to your personal information, such as medical or financial records;
- having personal information about your private life kept confidential.

For people with learning disabilities, because they often rely on the support of other people to live their lives, the right to respect for private life can be especially important. It includes a right to personal autonomy – making their own choices about their life and having support with this – and human dignity. For people with learning disabilities, the right to respect for their private life may be particularly relevant for the following reasons:

- *Privacy concerning their body*: who sees and touches your body is a fundamental part of private life.
- *Personal and sexual relationships*: people with learning disabilities have the same right as anyone to have relationships.

- *Taking part in community life*: this means being able to enjoy the same access to work, social, cultural and recreational activities as everyone else.

- *Abortion*: a woman with learning disabilities has the right to make her own choices about whether or not to keep her baby, unless she lacks capacity to make this decision.

- *Decisions about treatment*: provided a person with learning disabilities has the legal capacity to make a decision about a particular treatment then they have the right to decide whether to go ahead with medical treatment.

Taking part in community life means being able to enjoy the same access to social activites as everyone else.

An important part of your job is helping the person you support to understand their human rights and to support them to know when their rights are being breached or are at risk of being breached. You can do this by using accessible materials, DVDs and giving the person information about local advocacy services if they don't already have them. An equally important part of your job is to do all you can to uphold that person's human rights if they are at risk of being breached.

Activity

Can you think of any ways in which a person you support does not have their private life respected? What steps could you take to ensure their private life is respected? Discuss your ideas with your manager at your next supervision.

Respect for home

This is not a right to housing but rather a right to respect for the home you already have. For people with learning disabilities, this right can be especially important if circumstances mean they have to leave their own home. In order to ensure respect for a person with learning disabilities' right to their home, public authorities must take their needs into account and any action taken must be justified as lawful, necessary and proportionate. It is important that you support the person to have their voice heard and their needs recognised. Using person centred approaches and planning are particularly important in such a situation. Make sure the person has a person centred assessment that identifies their support needs and ways to address them.

The right to life

This says that public authorities:

- *must not take away a person's life* except in a few very limited circumstances;

- *must take reasonable steps to protect a person's life.*

The duty to protect life does not mean that everything possible must always be done to save life. Sometimes helping someone to live longer means they suffer so much it is not fair to keep trying to save their life. As long as the person has capacity (that is, they are able to make a decision for themselves at the time when the decision needs to be made), the person must give consent (agree) before they are allowed to die. As a learning disability worker you may be involved in issues relating to the right to life when you are supporting a person who is seriously ill or when consent to treatment is needed. To support the person in such situations you will need to work closely with other people, such as their family and friends, their doctor and other medical staff, and their advocate. Your organisation's policies and procedures will explain what you should do.

The right not to be discriminated against

This is discrimination that happens when a person with learning disabilities can show that they have been treated in a different way compared with someone else in a similar position.

> **Activity**
>
> **Familiarising yourself with the Human Rights Act** Use the internet or a library to familiarise yourself with the Human Rights Act and find out more about how it relates to the lives of people with learning disabilities. At a supervision or team meeting, share what you find out.

The Mental Capacity Act 2005

The Mental Capacity Act is an important law for people with learning disabilities in England and Wales and one that you need to know and understand clearly if you are to support people with learning disabilities effectively. In Scotland the relevant law is the Adults with Incapacity (Scotland) Act 2000; in Northern Ireland mental health issues are currently dealt with under common law although there are plans to introduce capacity legislation. The Mental Capacity Act provides a legal framework for acting and making decisions for people aged 16 or over who are unable to make such decisions themselves. The kind of decisions the Mental Capacity Act covers includes decisions relating to health, welfare, finance and property.

The Mental Capacity Act says that people have capacity unless it can be shown that they cannot make their own decisions. This is important for people with learning disabilities because people often presume they do not have capacity.

> It should be assumed that an adult (aged 16 or over) has full legal capacity to make decisions for themselves (the right to autonomy) unless it can be shown that they lack capacity to make a decision for themselves at the time that the decision needs to be made

Mental Capacity Act 2005, Code of Practice 1.2

The Mental Capacity Act also says that an individual can only be treated as unable to make a decision if all practical steps to help them make the decision have been taken. When the person is judged to lack capacity to make that particular decision, the decision which is made for them must be made in their best interests and also be made in a way that is least restricting of their rights and freedom of action.

Some individuals who lack capacity may also have no family or friends who would be appropriate to talk to about important decisions. When certain types of decisions are being made, NHS services and local authorities must make sure that an advocate is appointed to represent and support the person. An advocate is an independent person who can speak up for an individual with learning disabilities or help them to speak up for themselves. This includes decisions about:

- serious medical treatment;

- changes of accommodation;

- care reviews;

- adult protection cases.

The important things for you to remember about the law and capacity issues are:

- all adults are presumed to have capacity to make decisions;

- a person may only be treated as unable to make a decision if all practical steps to help them make the decision have been taken;

- any decision made on the person's behalf must be made in their best interests after a sharing of views by people who know the person well, for example their family and friends, or workers who have known them a long time;

- any decision made on the person's behalf must be made in a way that is least restricting of their rights and freedom of action;

- a person who lacks capacity and also has no family or friends who would be appropriate to ask about important decisions should be represented and supported by an advocate.

For more information about supporting people to make decisions about treatment, see the BILD book a *Brief Guide to the Mental Capacity Act 2005: Implications for people with learning disabilities* by Elaine Hardie and Liz Brooks.

Activity

Familiarising yourself with the capacity legislation in your country

Use the internet or a local library to familiarise yourself with the Mental Capacity Act, or the relevant laws in your country, and find out more about how it relates to the lives of the people with learning disabilities you support. Or go on a training day about capacity issues. At a supervision or team meeting, share what you find out.

Consider how you support people with day-to-day choices as well as how you might support a person who lacks capacity.

Activity

Find out from your line manager about the arrangements in your organisation for supporting people with decision making and for assessing capacity. Also find out how family carers are involved and have access to information so that they can be supported if they are partners in making a best interest decision.

The Equality Act 2010

The Equality Act 2010 brings together under one law all previous laws about discrimination in Britain. (In Northern Ireland, which is not covered by the Equality Act, people will have less protection against unlawful discrimination, harassment and victimisation until the law there is changed.) The Equality Act provides legal protection against discrimination under six main equality strands:

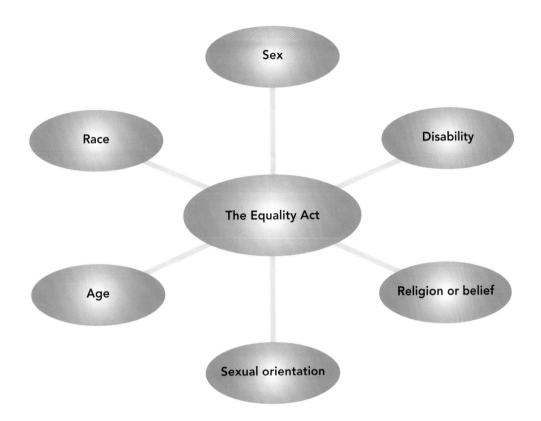

The six main equality strands are:

- sex;
- race;
- disability;
- age;
- religion or belief;
- sexual orientation.

In terms of disability discrimination, the Equality Act 2010 replaces the Disability Discrimination Acts 1995 and 2005. For people with learning disabilities and those who support them, the Act also introduces some changes:

- It protects a person from being discriminated against because they are linked or associated with a person with disabilities. This new protection could be important for family carers and for you as a learning disability worker. It would make it unlawful for a business or service provider to discriminate against a family carer or you because you are with or associated with a person or people with learning disabilities.

- Direct discrimination against people with disabilities is now unlawful not only in the workplace but when individuals are accessing goods and services. For example, a pub or restaurant cannot refuse to serve a person because they may need support to eat.

- It is unlawful to discriminate against an individual because of something connected with their disability. This is called discrimination arising from disability. An example would be telling a man with a hearing impairment that he cannot stay in a hotel because he would not be able to hear the fire alarm.

- It is now unlawful to cause indirect discrimination. This is when there is a rule, policy or even practice that is for everyone but that makes things harder for people with a disability.

- Disability harassment is now unlawful. This is when someone's behaviour violates a disabled person's dignity or creates an environment for them that is intimidating, hostile, degrading, humiliating or offensive. For example, calling someone with a disability names or bullying them because they have a disability.

Organisational policies and procedures

When you start a new job, you should receive induction training during which you are made aware of all your organisation's policies and procedures. If you work as a personal assistant you too should receive induction training and you should find out from your employer whether they have policies and procedures for their staff or if they have agreed the ways that you should support them, such as through a contract of employment or supervision.

Wherever you work your induction is the time when you need to make sure you properly understand your role and responsibilities, especially in terms of what to do and who to go to if you have concerns about the rights of the person you support. If you feel you do not understand the policies and procedures, or agreed ways of working, or you need more information about your role and responsibilities, talk to your line manager about it in supervision. Don't be afraid to ask questions, as it is important you know and understand what to do if you have concerns.

You can find more information about the Equality Act from the Equality and Human Rights Commission's website at www.equalityhumanrights.com and in the book *Equality and Inclusion for Learning Disability Workers* by Rorie Fulton and Kate Richardson in this series.

Other important policies and legislation
Safeguarding adults

Research shows us that people with learning disabilities are more likely to suffer abuse than other members of society because of a wide range of reasons. It might be that they don't realise that they are being abused, or they might not be able to communicate with others what is happening to them or that they are dependent on their abuser and have been threatened in some way not to tell. Therefore it is the responsibility of everyone who works with people who have a learning disability to be aware that abuse happens, and to know what to do if they think that someone is being abused.

Safeguarding adults, or protection of vulnerable adults as it used to be called, is an important policy in your workplace. This policy will tell you what the signs of potential abuse are so that you can recognise it, and it will tell you what your role is when you do spot the signs of abuse.

This policy is based on a number of different pieces of national policy and legislation, with each of the four nations of the UK having their own version of this legislation. Whilst the legislation may differ from country to country the main principles and themes remain the same for all four nations.

Some of the pieces of legislation are outlined below:

- *No Secrets* **(2000)** was the first government guidance in England on the protection of vulnerable adults. It explains that when safeguarding people, working together is essential for all professionals , including care workers, managers, social workers, health staff and police. Every care service in your local area will also follow the same procedure to make sure that everyone works in the same way.

- **Safeguarding Vulnerable Groups Act (2006)** (England) has introduced the new Independent Safeguarding Authority (ISA), which means that everyone working with vulnerable adults will need to be registered with the ISA to work within this area. This is an extra safeguard to ensure that people who are abusers cannot access the most vulnerable people within society.

- In Scotland, the **Adult Support and Protection (Scotland) Act 2007** and the **Protection of Vulnerable Groups (Scotland) Act 2007,** and in Wales the **Safeguarding Vulnerable Groups Act 2006 (Controlled Activity) (Wales) Regulations 2010** have been put in place to protect vulnerable adults, including people with learning disabilities.

> ### Thinking point
>
> *We all feel vulnerable at some time in our lives, when we are ill, or are having a difficult time in our lives. Imagine how much more vulnerable we might feel if we couldn't communicate with other people; if we were dependent upon others to make our food, or take us to the toilet and get us dressed; or if we couldn't understand what was happening to us or why it was happening.*

What does this mean for the person with a learning disability?

These pieces of legislation and national policy mean that staff who work with people who have a learning disability are aware of what abuse is, what the signs and symptoms are, what their role is and what they have to do if they suspect abuse. The person with a learning disability can be reassured that they will be taken seriously and that they are supported if they are being abused. Also they can be sure that they will be kept safe, as all support workers have to have a criminal records check.

Confidentiality

People with a learning disability deserve the respect and privacy we expect for ourselves, and people in a paid capacity don't have an automatic right to know personal information about the people they support, only the parts that they need to. Your workplace will have a policy about confidentiality. This is to make sure you know what information you can or cannot share, and with which people and when you can share it. One way of saying this to help others understand what it means in practice is to say, *'what's said in the room – stays in the room'.*

The **Data Protection Act (2003)** covers the UK and it sets out the rules for how information that is held about an individual should be used in a lawful way. This Act will inform how you handle confidential information about a person you support. There is more information about this Act in the book *Handling Information for Learning Disability Workers* by Lesley Barcham and Jackie Pountney in this series.

Key points from this chapter

- Each of the four countries in the UK has a policy on supporting people with a learning disability.

- The Human Rights Act is based on the FREDA values: fairness, respect, equality, dignity and autonomy.

- The Equality Act 2010 replaces the earlier legislation on disability discrimination and discrimination on the grounds of age, gender or ethnic origin.

- It is important to remember that the laws on capacity in England, Wales and Scotland assume that all adults are presumed to have capacity to make decisions.

References and where to go for more information

References

Barcham, L and Pountney, J (2011) *Handling Information for Learning Disability Workers.* Exeter: Learning Matters and BILD

Bickerton, S (2011) *Principles of Safeguarding and Protection for Learning Disability Workers.* Exeter: Learning Matters and BILD

British Institute of Human Rights (2008) *Your Human Rights – A guide for disabled people.* London: BIHR

Department for Constitutional Affairs (2006) *A Guide to the Human Rights Act 1998; Third Edition.* London: TSO

Finnegan, P and Clarke, S (2005) *One Law for All? The impact of the human rights act on people with learning disabilities.* London: VIA

Fulton, R and Richardson, K (2011) *Equality and Inclusion for Learning Disability Workers.* Exeter: Learning Matters and BILD

Hardie, E and Brooks, L (2009) *Brief Guide to the Mental Capacity Act.* Kidderminster: BILD

Mansell, J, Brown, J B et al. (2005) *Person-centred Active Support.* Brighton: Pavilion

Ministry of Justice (2008) *A Guide to the Human Rights Act: A booklet for people with learning disabilities*, available from www.justice.gov.uk

Legislation, policies and reports

Department of Health (2001) *Valuing People: A new strategy for learning disability for the 21st century.* London: The Stationery Office

Department of Health (2009) *Valuing People Now.* London: Department of Health

Department of Health, Social Services and Public Safety (2005) *Equal Lives: Review of policy and services for people with a learning disability in Northern Ireland.* Belfast: Department of Health, Social Services and Public Safety

Report of the National Assembly of Wales (2007) *The Statement on Policy and Practice for Adults with a Learning Disability.* Welsh Assembly Government

Scottish Executive (2000) *The Same As You? A review of services for people with learning disabilities.* Edinburgh: Scottish Executive

The Mental Capacity Act is used in England and Wales. In Scotland, the Adults with Incapacity (Scotland) Act 2000 applies – further information can be found on www.scotland.gov.uk. Ireland currently has no specific legislation around mental capacity.

Human Rights Act 1998

Equality Act 2010

Websites

Ann Craft Trust www.anncrafttrust.org

BILD www.bild.org.uk

British Institute of Human Rights www.bihr.org.uk

Equality and Human Rights Commission www.equalityhumanrights.com

Foundation for People with Learning Disabilities www.learningdisabilities.org.uk/

Mencap www.mencap.org.uk

Sense – UK Deafblind Charity (and associated disabilities) www.sense.org.uk

Valuing People www.valuingpeoplenow.dh.gov.uk

Glossary

Abuse – a violation of a person's human and civil rights by any other person or persons, which usually involves a misuse of power.

Advocacy – helping and supporting someone else to speak up for what they want.

Age appropriate – means the communication or activity should be right for the age of the person who you support.

Active participation – a way of working that recognises an individual's right to participate in the activities and relationships of everyday life as independently as possible. The person is an active partner in their own support rather than a passive recipient of care.

Asylum – originally meant a place of refuge or safety.

Breach – if your human rights are breached, it means they are ignored.

Citizen advocate – a member of the public who volunteers to support someone to speak up for themselves.

Communication – the way that two or more people make contact, build relationships and share messages. These messages can be ideas, thoughts or feelings as well as information and questions. Communication involves both sending and understanding these messages and can be done through many different ways including speech, writing, drawing, pictures, symbols, signs, pointing and body language, for example.

Communication aids – these can range from simple boards or books to more sophisticated devices. They can use pictures or words or symbols. 'Voice output communication aids' are those that can be operated by eye gaze, switches, keyboards or touch screens to trigger spoken messages. A **Lightwriter** is an example of a voice output communication aid where the user types a message onto a keyboard.

Confidentiality – keeping some things private.

Consent – a person consents if he or she agrees by choice and has the freedom and capacity to make that choice.

Continuum of learning abilities – an idea used to explain the wide range of abilities to learn found in the population.

Day centre – a place people can attend, often during the day, to meet other people, have a meal and take part in activities. Day centres can be run by local authorities or independent or voluntary sector providers.

Duty of care – those in a professional or other paid capacity, with responsibility for providing support to others, must take reasonable care to avoid acts or omissions that are likely to cause harm to the person or persons they care for or to other people.

Empower – to enable an individual to take action to control their own lives.

Eugenics movement – a movement popular in the late nineteenth and earlier twentieth century which focused on the science of improving the human race by controlling inherited characteristics.

Family carer – a relative of a person with learning disabilities who has an interest in their wellbeing.

Informed decision – an informed decision is one where a choice is made by an individual, using relevant information about the advantages and disadvantages of all the possible courses of action.

Intellectual disability – a term used increasingly in other English speaking countries, such as America, Canada and Australia, meaning the same as the term learning disability used in the UK.

IQ tests – (or intelligence quotient tests) are administered by psychologists to produce a statistical score for a person in relation to their intelligence. In the past these were often used to diagnose a person's learning disability. Today assessments of the person's daily living skills are considered more useful in assessing the impact of any learning disability on the person.

Issue based advocacy – often used when a person has an important decision to make and they need support to understand the choices available to them and what rights they have.

Independent Mental Capacity Advocate (IMCA) – an IMCA safeguards the rights of people who are facing a decision about a long-term move or about a serious medical treatment and who lack capacity to make a specified decision at the time it needs to be made. IMCAs support people who have nobody else who is willing and able to represent them or be consulted in the process of working out their best interests, other than paid staff.

Learning difficulties – many people with a learning disability prefer the term learning difficulties because they want to get across the idea that their learning support needs change over time.

Labels – the term 'learning disability' is a label that is used as a convenience in discussions and planning, for example in health and social care. The reality is that someone who may have the label of having a learning disability will also have other labels such as wife, sister or friend. A label only describes one aspect of a person.

Learning disabilities – a learning disability is an impairment that starts before adulthood and that has a lasting effect on the person's development. It includes the presence of a significantly reduced ability to understand new or complex information or to learn new skills. It also means having a reduced ability to cope independently.

Legislation – the laws that cover a particular area.

Mental capacity – a person's ability to make their own decisions and to understand the consequences of those decisions.

Models of disability – how we see the place of people with disabilities in society and how we respond to them.

Non-verbal communication – communication that does not use words but uses gesture, body language, signing, symbols, objects of reference and other communication aids.

Normalisation – a set of principles, developed by Wolf Wolfensberger, which says that people with a learning disability should live in ordinary places, doing ordinary things, with other people: essentially experiencing the 'normal' patterns of everyday life.

Objects of reference – a way to communicate using objects to represent words and ideas. Objects of reference are often used for people who cannot either see or understand pictures. For example, showing a person a mug to ask whether they want a drink of tea.

Ordinary life principles – supported by the Kings Fund in the 1980s, their project *An Ordinary Life* promoted the idea that people with learning disabilities should live their lives in the community in ordinary homes.

Peer advocacy – when a person with a learning disability supports another person with a learning disability to speak up for themselves.

Pre natal – before birth.

Peri natal – during birth.

Post natal – after birth.

Person centred planning – a structured way to make sure that people with learning disabilities are at the centre of all planning, choices and discussions about their life. Person centred planning helps them to live their lives in their own way and to meet their wishes and dreams.

Personal assistants – a term often used to describe people employed directly by a person to provide care and support (such as through direct payments or an individual budget).

Personalisation – starting with the person as an individual with strengths, preferences and aspirations and putting them at the centre of the process of identifying their needs and making choices about how and when they are supported to live their lives.

Person centred approaches – a way of working every day with people with learning disabilities that puts the person and their dreams at the centre of everything you do.

Policy – a plan or statement (from a government or an organisation) describing how they will work towards their aims and objectives on a particular issue.

Procedure – a set of instructions which sets out in detail how a policy should be implemented and what staff should do in response to a specific situation.

Public authorities – organisations such as the government, social services, schools and hospitals.

Public services – services which the government provides such as social services, hospitals, and schools.

Rights – a framework of laws that protects people from harm, sets out what people can say and do and guarantees the right to a fair trial and other basic entitlements, such as the right to respect and equality.

Safeguarding – helping to protect vulnerable people from abuse by others.

Self advocacy – self advocacy groups are for people with learning difficulties to meet, find out about their rights, share their experiences and support each other to speak up.

Service – the provision of social care support for a person that could be in their own home, their local community, a residential home or similar place.

Signs – hand gestures that are used in an agreed way to communicate. Signs from British Sign Language (BSL) have been used in several vocabularies specifically for people with learning disabilities, such as Makaton and Signalong.

Social inclusion – when individuals with a learning disability are included and involved in everyday life, and so have the same life chances as other members of society.

Social role valorisation – a concept developed by Wolf Wolfensberger, which suggests that attention should be given to countering poor attitudes towards people with disabilities by helping them to take on valued social roles, for example as family members, neighbours and employees.

Staff – people employed on a paid or unpaid (voluntary) basis by an organisation to organise and deliver its services.

Support plan – detailed plan of a person's support needs that support workers should use to inform their day-to-day support for that individual.

Symbols – line drawings that are used in an agreed way to communicate. There are many different symbols systems designed for use with people with learning disabilities including Widget Rebus and Makaton. There are black and white or coloured symbols.

Verbal communication – communication that uses words (either spoken or written).

Index

Added to a page number 'g' denotes glossary.

Quick

KIDS' CAKES

Sara Lewis

Quick & easy
KIDS' CAKES

50 great cakes for children of all ages

hamlyn

First published in Great Britain in 2006 by Hamlyn, a division of
Octopus Publishing Group Ltd, 2–4 Heron Quays, London E14 4JP

ISBN-13: 978-0-600-61493-7
ISBN-10: 0-600-61493-X

A CIP catalogue record for this book is available from the British Library

Printed and bound in China

10 9 8 7 6 5 4 3 2 1

Dedication
For Nicky and her powers of persuasion.

Notes
Standard level spoon measurements are used in all recipes.
1 tablespoon = one 15 ml spoon
1 teaspoon = one 5 ml spoon

Medium eggs should be used unless otherwise stated.

Both metric and imperial measurements have been given. Use one
set of measurements only, and not a mixture of both.

Ovens should be preheated to the specified temperature – if using a
fan-assisted oven, follow the manufacturer's instructions for adjusting
the time and the temperature.

Contents

Introduction

For young children or the young at heart, nothing beats the thrill of blowing out the candles on your birthday cake, but as a busy working parent, the idea of finding the time to make a cake that is extra special can fill you with horror.

Over the next few pages, you will find 50 quick and easy cakes to delight tiny tots and melt the heart of even the coolest older child. Some can be decorated in 20 minutes or so, while others will take around an hour. The cakes may be baked and frozen in advance to spread the workload, and most can be made with equipment that you will already have in your kitchen cupboards. Alternatively, cheat and buy a plain cake from your local supermarket. All cakes can be made by even the most inexperienced of cake makers – you may just find that it takes you a few minutes longer to do. Don't be put off if you have never made a cake before. If you can roll out frozen pastry, you can roll out and cover a cake with ready-to-roll icing. Very often it is the simplest cake that is the most eye-catching.

In the first section of the book, you will find all the basic recipes for making the cakes themselves, with tips on flavour variations, recipes for different icings and fillings, plus advice and techniques on achieving that special finish. The main section features cake designs for both younger and older children, boys and girls, decorated with butter icing, ready-to-roll icing, chocolate and sweets. There is something for everyone, from a cute pastel-coloured tortoise to an inviting white chocolate puppy; from jewelled pink crowns or mini birthday cakes to a sweet-guzzling monster, a grown-up game of chess and a scary ghostly face.

But you don't have to wait for a birthday to try these cakes. They make great school raffle prizes or can simply be made with the children as a fun way to cheer up a dreary day in the school holidays. Whatever the occasion, making and decorating your own cake is a great way to show just how much you care.

Equipment

The recipes in this book are generally quick and easy to make and assemble, so the amount of equipment you will need is minimal. You will probably find that you already have most of the items of equipment you need, with perhaps the exception of some of the more specialist tiny icing cutters. If you are new to cake making, it is worth checking which tins are required before you begin baking so that you are not disappointed.

If there is a piece of equipment you need to buy, it's well worth visiting your local cake-decorating shop. They are usually packed with cutters, tools, ready-made decorations, coloured icings and almost every shade of food colouring imaginable. However, if you don't have a convenient local shop, you will find that many of the larger kitchenware companies offer a comprehensive mail-order service.

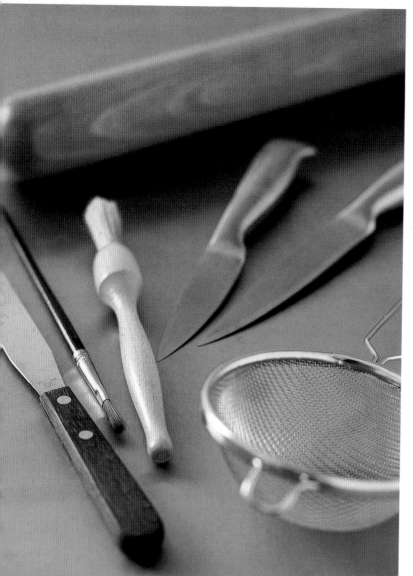

BASIC EQUIPMENT

- kitchen scales
- baking tins
- greaseproof paper and nonstick baking paper
- paper cake cases
- scissors
- pastry brush
- artists' paintbrushes
- selection of bowls in various sizes
- large and small sieve – a new tea strainer is ideal
- large serrated knife for cutting cakes in half, round-bladed knife for spreading butter icing, large and small cook's knives for cutting icing shapes
- large and small palette knives
- large and small rolling pins
- whisk
- biscuit cutters and selection of small/mini cutters

Tip

If you like cooking, the chances are that you will already have most of the equipment that you need, with the exception of specialist cutters or cake boards.

CAKE TINS

Most cake tins can be found in the cookware department of your local large department store or hardware shop or large supermarket. For more unusual equipment, visit a specialist cookware or cake-decorating shop, or check out appropriate websites on the Internet. If buying new tins, opt for the better-quality ranges, as they will last for 20 years or more without denting or warping. A loose-bottomed tin makes it easier to remove a cake, but is not essential. Likewise, flexible muffin and fairy cake moulds are easy to use, but rigid metal ones work just as well.

MOST FREQUENTLY USED CAKE TINS

- 23 cm (9 inch) deep round tin
- 20 cm (8 inch) deep square tin
- 2 x 20 cm (8 inch) straight-sided sandwich tins
- 18 cm (7 inch) deep round tin
- 12-section bun tray
- 30 x 23 x 5 cm (12 x 9 x 2 inch) roasting tin

Lining a deep round tin

Brush the sides and base of the tin lightly with a little oil, then cut strips of greaseproof paper a little taller than the side of the tin. Fold a strip about 1 cm (½ inch) in from one long edge, then snip up to the fold line at intervals. Stand the paper in the tin so that the cut edges sit flat on the base of the tin. Cut and add extra paper strips, overlapping the ends of the strips slightly, as necessary to cover the entire side of the tin. Using the tin as a guide, stand it on some more greaseproof paper, draw around the tin, then cut out the round and press on to the base of the tin. Brush the paper lightly with more oil. If using nonstick baking paper instead of greaseproof paper, simply add the paper shapes to the dry tin.

Lining a deep square tin

Cut strips of paper a little taller than the sides of the tin, just as when lining a round tin, but snip up to the fold line only where the paper is pressed into the corners of the tin. Cut a square of paper for the base in just the same way as for a round tin.

Lining a roasting tin

Cut a piece of nonstick baking paper a little larger than the tin, then make diagonal cuts into the corners. Press the paper into the tin, tucking the snipped edges one behind the other so that the base and sides of the tin are completely lined in one action. You can use greaseproof paper instead of nonstick baking paper, but you will need to grease both the tin and the paper.

Lining a sandwich tin

Brush the base and side of the tin with a little oil, then stand the tin on top of a piece of greaseproof paper, draw around the tin and cut out the round of paper. Lay over the base of the tin and brush lightly with a little extra oil.

Cake recipes

Most of the cakes in this book are based on two simple cake mixes: a Madeira cake and a quick-mix sandwich cake. These mixtures are then baked in a variety of different items of bakeware – you'll be surprised to find just how many shapes can be conjured up from a few cake tins, pudding basins, the odd mixing bowl and a roasting tin. Make and bake the cake the day before the party or freeze it a week or so in advance, un-iced. This section also includes recipes for individual cakes – fairy cakes and muffins – plus a Swiss roll. For people short of time, shop-bought equivalents have been listed, where available, on main recipes.

MADEIRA CAKES

This traditional creamed cake is made by beating butter or soft margarine with sugar until light and fluffy. Gradually mix in beaten eggs and self-raising flour until smooth. Alternating eggs and flour will prevent the eggs curdling or separating the mixture. Unlike an all-in-one cake, this has a greater proportion of flour to fat and sugar and produces a light, slightly closer-textured cake that can be cut and shaped well, making it ideal for that special birthday cake.

Small Madeira Cake

175 g (6 oz) soft margarine or butter, at room temperature

175 g (6 oz) caster sugar

3 eggs

1 tablespoon milk

225 g (7½ oz) self-raising flour

FLAVOURINGS

Vanilla 1 teaspoon vanilla extract

Lemon grated rind of ¾ lemon; replace milk with 1 tablespoon lemon juice

Orange grated rind of ¾ orange; replace milk with 1 tablespoon orange juice

Chocolate replace 50 g (2 oz) flour with same weight of cocoa powder

The above amount will fill:

SIZE OF CONTAINER	BAKING TIME
18 cm (7 inch) deep round cake tin	45–50 minutes
15 cm (6 inch) deep square cake tin	45–50 minutes
20 cm (8 inch) mixing bowl	50–60 minutes
1.2 litre (2 pint) pudding basin	1 hour 10 minutes

Medium Madeira Cake

250 g (8 oz) soft margarine or butter, at room temperature

250 g (8 oz) caster sugar

4 eggs

2 tablespoons milk

300 g (10 oz) self-raising flour

1 teaspoon baking powder (for roasting tin cake only)

FLAVOURINGS

Vanilla **2 teaspoons vanilla extract**

Lemon **grated rind of 1 lemon; replace milk with 2 tablespoons lemon juice**

Orange **grated rind of 1 orange; replace milk with 2 tablespoons orange juice**

Chocolate **replace 65 g (2½ oz) flour with same weight of cocoa powder**

The above amount will fill:

SIZE OF CONTAINER	BAKING TIME
30 x 23 x 5 cm (12 x 9 x 2 inch) roasting tin	30–35 minutes
1.5 litre (2½ pint) pudding basin	1¼–1½ hours
2 x 900 ml (1½ pint) pudding basins	about 1 hour
1.2 litre (2 pint) and 750 ml (1¼ pint) pudding basins	1 hour 5 minutes – 1hour 10 minutes for larger basin cake, 55–60 minutes for smaller basin cake
20 cm (8 inch) single sandwich tin cake and 900 ml (1½ pint) pudding basin	30 minutes for sandwich cake, about 1 hour for basin cake

Large Madeira Cake

375 g (12 oz) soft margarine or butter, at room temperature

375 g (12 oz) caster sugar

6 eggs

4 tablespoons milk

625 g (1¼ lb) self-raising flour

FLAVOURINGS

Vanilla **3 teaspoons vanilla extract**

Lemon **grated rind of 2 lemons; replace milk with 4 tablespoons lemon juice**

Orange **grated rind of 2 oranges; replace milk with 4 tablespoons orange juice**

Chocolate **replace 100 g (3½ oz) flour with same weight of cocoa powder**

The above amount will fill:

SIZE OF CONTAINER	BAKING TIME
23 cm (9 inch) deep round cake tin	1–1¼ hours
20 cm (8 inch) deep square cake tin	1–1¼ hours

1 Cream the margarine or butter and sugar together in a bowl until light and fluffy. Beat the eggs and milk, or eggs only if you are making a fruit-flavoured cake, in a small bowl with a fork. Mix the flour with the cocoa powder and baking powder, if using, in a separate small bowl. Add alternate spoonfuls of the egg mixture and flour and beat into the creamed mixture until they have all been incorporated and the cake mixture is smooth. Beat in the vanilla extract or grated lemon or orange rind and juice, if using.

2 Spoon the cake mixture into your chosen greased and lined tin. Bake in a preheated oven, 160°C (325°F), Gas Mark 3, for the appropriate time (see boxed text), until well risen and golden brown and a skewer comes out of the centre of the cake cleanly (see page 19). Leave for 10 minutes in the tin, then loosen the edges with a palette knife, turn out on to a wire rack and leave to cool completely.

QUICK-MIX CAKES

This is a quick and easy all-in-one cake that can be made in minutes and may be used for varying-sized sandwich cakes and fairy cakes. Quite simply, all the ingredients are put into the bowl at the same time and beaten for just a few minutes until smooth and creamy. If you are using butter, the secret is to have it at room temperature so that it will beat easily either with a wooden spoon, electric mixer or food processor. As the mixing time is so brief, a little baking powder is added to boost the raising agent in the self-raising flour and to guarantee success every time.

Large round Quick-mix Sandwich Cake

250 g (8 oz) soft margarine

250 g (8 oz) caster sugar

250 g (8 oz) self-raising flour

1 teaspoon baking powder

4 eggs

FLAVOURINGS

Vanilla **1 teaspoon vanilla extract**

Lemon **grated rind of 1 lemon**

Orange **grated rind of 1 small orange**

Chocolate **replace 40 g (1½ oz) flour with same weight of cocoa powder**

1 Put all the ingredients into a bowl, with your chosen flavouring, if using, and beat together until smooth.

2 Spoon the cake mixture into 2 x 20 cm (8 inch) greased and base-lined sandwich tins (see page 11).

3 Bake in a preheated oven, 180°C (350°F), Gas Mark 4, for about 25 minutes until springy to the touch (see page 19). Leave for 5 minutes in the tins, then turn out on to a wire rack and leave to cool completely.

Medium round Quick-mix Sandwich Cake

175 g (6 oz) soft margarine

175 g (6 oz) caster sugar

175 g (6 oz) self-raising flour

½ teaspoon baking powder

3 eggs

FLAVOURINGS

Vanilla **¾ teaspoon vanilla extract**

Lemon **grated rind of ¾ lemon**

Orange **grated rind of ¾ small orange**

Chocolate **replace 25 g (1 oz) flour with same weight of cocoa powder**

1 Put all the ingredients into a bowl, with your chosen flavouring, if using, and beat together until smooth.

2 Spoon the cake mixture into 2 x 18 cm (7 inch) greased and base-lined sandwich tins (see page 11).

3 Bake in a preheated oven, 180°C (350°F), Gas Mark 4, for about 20 minutes until springy to the touch (see page 19). Leave for 5 minutes in the tins, then turn out on to a wire rack and leave to cool completely.

Small round Quick-mix Sandwich Cake

125 g (4 oz) soft margarine

125 g (4 oz) caster sugar

125 g (4 oz) self-raising flour

¼ teaspoon baking powder

2 eggs

FLAVOURINGS

Vanilla ½ teaspoon vanilla extract

Lemon grated rind of ½ lemon

Orange grated rind of ½ small orange

Chocolate replace 2 tablespoons flour with
the same weight of cocoa powder

1 Put all the ingredients into a bowl,
with your chosen flavouring, if using,
and beat together until smooth.

2 Spoon the cake mixture into 2 x
15 cm (6 inch) greased and base-
lined sandwich tins (see page 11).

3 Bake in a preheated oven, 180°C
(350°F), Gas Mark 4, for about
15 minutes until springy to the touch
(see page 19). Leave for 5 minutes in
the tins, then turn out on to a wire
rack and leave to cool completely.

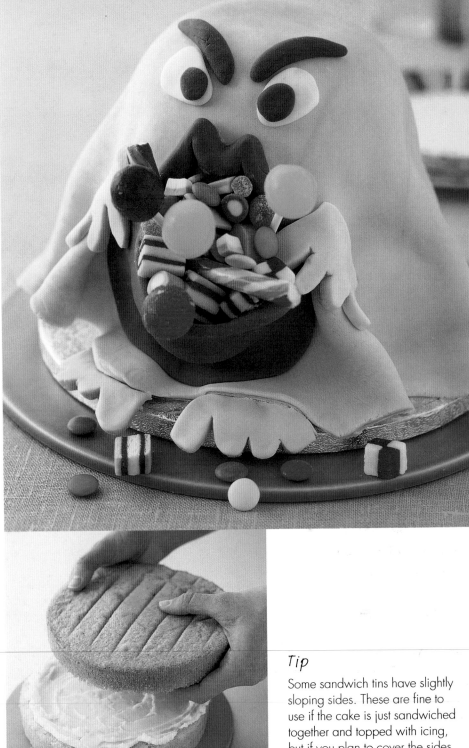

Tip

Some sandwich tins have slightly
sloping sides. These are fine to
use if the cake is just sandwiched
together and topped with icing,
but if you plan to cover the sides
of the cake with icing, you will
need straight-sided tins, otherwise
the finished cake will have an
unsatisfactory appearance.

Fairy Cakes
Makes 12

125 g (4 oz) soft margarine

125 g (4 oz) caster sugar

125 g (4 oz) self-raising flour

2 eggs

FLAVOURINGS

Vanilla ½ teaspoon vanilla extract

Lemon grated rind of ½ lemon

Orange grated rind of ½ small orange

Chocolate replace 2 tablespoons flour with same weight of cocoa powder

1 Line a 12-section bun tray with paper cake cases. Put all the ingredients into a bowl, with your chosen flavouring, if using, and beat together until smooth.

2 Divide the cake mixture evenly between the paper cake cases using a dessertspoon and level the surface.

3 Bake in a preheated oven, 180°C (350°F), Gas Mark 4, for 15 minutes until springy to the touch (see page 19). Leave for 5 minutes in the tray, then remove cakes to a wire rack and leave to cool completely.

Shallow Cake

50 g (2 oz) soft margarine

50 g (2 oz) caster sugar

50 g (2 oz) self-raising flour

⅛ teaspoon baking powder

1 egg

1 Put all the ingredients into a bowl and beat together with a wooden spoon or an electric mixer until smooth.

2 Spoon into an 18 cm (7 inch) greased and base-lined sandwich tin (see page 11).

3 Bake in a preheated oven, 180°C (350°F), Gas Mark 4, for 12–15 minutes until springy to the touch (see page 19). Leave for 5 minutes in the tin, then turn out on to a wire rack and leave to cool completely.

MUFFINS
Makes 12

300 g (10 oz) plain flour

3 teaspoons baking powder

125 g (4 oz) light muscovado sugar

3 eggs

4 tablespoons sunflower oil

50 g (2 oz) butter, melted

150 g (5 oz) natural yogurt

FLAVOURINGS

Vanilla **2 teaspoons vanilla extract**

Chocolate **replace 40 g (1½ oz) flour with same weight of cocoa powder**

Double chocolate **replace 40 g (1½ oz) flour with same weight of cocoa powder and add 100 g (3½ oz) diced milk chocolate**

1 Line a 12-section deep muffin tray with paper cake cases. Put all the ingredients into a bowl, with your chosen flavouring, if using, and combine with a fork until only just mixed.

2 Divide the muffin mixture evenly between the paper cases using a dessertspoon.

3 Bake the muffins in a preheated oven, 190°C (375°F), Gas Mark 5, for 18–20 minutes until they are well risen and the tops are golden brown and have cracked slightly. Leave for 5 minutes in the tray, then remove cakes to a wire rack and leave to cool completely.

SWISS ROLL

Makes one 28 cm (11 inch) long Swiss roll

4 large eggs

125 g (4 oz) caster sugar, plus extra for sprinkling

125 g (4 oz) plain flour

1 tablespoon hot water

8 tablespoons raspberry or strawberry jam

FLAVOURING

Chocolate **replace 25 g (1 oz) flour with the same weight of cocoa powder and use chocolate spread in place of jam**

1 Line a 37 x 28 cm (15 x 11 inch) roasting tin with nonstick baking paper (see page 11), so that the paper stands about 2.5 cm (1 inch) high all around the sides. Put the eggs and sugar in a large heatproof bowl set over a saucepan of simmering water and whisk, ideally using a hand-held electric whisk, for about 10 minutes until very thick and pale and the mixture leaves a trail when the whisk is lifted just above the bowl.

2 Sift in the flour and use a large metal spoon to fold it into the egg mixture, adding the measured water once most of the flour is incorporated.

3 Turn the cake mixture into the tin and ease gently into the corners. Bake in a preheated oven, 200°C (400°F), Gas Mark 6, for 10–12 minutes until pale golden and just firm to the touch.

4 While the cake is baking, wet a clean tea towel with hot water, wring it out and put on the work surface so that the short edges are facing you. Cover with a sheet of greaseproof paper and sprinkle evenly with sugar.

5 Turn the cake out on to the paper and peel off the lining paper. Spread the cake with the jam, then roll up, starting from the short edge nearest to you. Put the Swiss roll, seam side down, on to a wire rack to cool.

IS MY CAKE COOKED?

If your cake looks well risen and brown but you are not sure if it is ready, there are several methods of checking it. Insert a skewer into the centre of a deep cake. If it comes out cleanly, it is ready, but if there is a smearing of cake mixture, put the cake back in the oven and test again at five- or ten-minute intervals, depending on how messy the skewer is.

For sandwich cakes and fairy cakes, press the top of the cake lightly with a fingertip. If the cake springs back, then it is ready. If the finger mark remains, then return the cake to the oven and test again in five minutes' time.

All ovens vary slightly, so use the timings as a guide and check shortly before the end of the baking time to see how your cake or cakes are doing. Resist the temptation to keep opening the oven, especially midway through cooking, or your cake will sink. If you have a fan-assisted oven, adjust the temperature slightly and reduce by 10°C (25°F), because these ovens can run hot. For larger cakes, check two-thirds of the way through the baking time and cover the top loosely with foil if the cake is browning too quickly.

SLICING THE TOP OFF A CAKE

With the exception of sandwich cakes, most cakes tend to peak during cooking and will need trimming before icing. The deeper the cake, the more it will rise in the centre. Trim the top level using a large serrated knife and then turn large cakes upside down before icing. Trim the tops of fairy cakes if spooning over glacé icing so that it will form a flat even layer and not run off the cake.

SHORT OF TIME?

Cheat and buy a cake from the supermarket. With lots of flavoured muffins, fairy cakes, Swiss rolls and filled sandwich cakes to choose from, it can be a lifesaver for a busy working mum. Look out for thick slices of plain or marbled Madeira cake and sandwich three or four side by side to make a larger square cake. Larger bought round sponge cakes may be more difficult to find, so buy whatever size you can and just scale the design down and make a slightly smaller version.

Icings and fillings

Some icings – including butter icing and ganache – are used as both a filling for a cake and as a delicious coating. Others, such as ready-to-roll icing, are used only as a cake covering. Refer to the individual recipes for guidance.

READY-TO-ROLL ICING

For speed, most of us will opt to buy this icing from the supermarket, but if you would prefer to make your own, it really is very easy. If you can't find liquid glucose – it is usually sold alongside the vanilla extract and other flavourings in supermarkets – then order it from your local chemist. Don't be tempted to leave it out, as it is crucial to the icing's elasticity. You will also find small boxes of dried egg white with the other baking ingredients in the supermarket, and, because it is pasteurized, it does not pose any potential health risk as in the case of raw egg white.

Makes 500 g (1 lb)

1 dried egg white

2 tablespoons liquid glucose

500 g (1 lb) icing sugar, sifted

1 Reconstitute the egg white with water according to the packet instructions.

2 Put the egg white into a large bowl with the liquid glucose, then gradually work in the sugar with a wooden spoon, kneading it with your hands straight on to the work surface when too stiff to stir. The mixture should be smooth and elastic, and you may find that you do not need to mix in all the sugar.

Tip

Ready-to-roll icing dries out quickly, so make sure that it is tightly wrapped in a plastic bag until you are ready to use it.

BUTTER ICING

Sometimes known as buttercream, this is a soft spreading icing that can be used plain or flavoured, spread smooth or roughed up or even coloured to fill and decorate cakes. For the best flavour, use good-quality unsalted butter at room temperature, or soften in the microwave, so that it is easy to mix with the icing sugar. A newly opened pack of icing sugar may be used straight from the pack, but if you have a pack that has been open a while, you may need to sift it before using to remove any lumps. Follow the method below and refer to the table for ingredient quantities and optional flavourings.

1 Put the butter into a bowl and soften with a wooden spoon or beat in a food processor.

2 Gradually beat in the sugar, then add the milk and/or your chosen flavouring, and mix to a soft spreading consistency.

QUANTITY	Single	One and a half	Double
unsalted butter, at room temperature	50 g (2 oz)	75 g (3 oz)	125 g (4 oz)
icing sugar	125 g (4 oz)	175 g (6 oz)	250 g (8 oz)
milk	1 teaspoon	2 teaspoons	1 tablespoon
FLAVOURINGS			
Vanilla	½ teaspoon vanilla extract	¾ teaspoon vanilla extract	1 teaspoon vanilla extract
Lemon	1 teaspoon grated lemon rind and 1 teaspoon lemon juice in place of milk	1½ teaspoons grated lemon rind and 2 teaspoons lemon juice in place of milk	2 teaspoons grated lemon rind and 1 tablespoon lemon juice in place of milk
Orange	1 teaspoon grated orange rind and 1 teaspoon orange juice in place of milk	1½ teaspoons grated orange rind and 2 teaspoons orange juice in place of milk	2 teaspoons grated orange rind and 1 tablespoon orange juice in place of milk
Chocolate	4 teaspoons cocoa powder dissolved in 2 teaspoons boiling water in place of milk	2 tablespoons cocoa powder dissolved in 4 teaspoons boiling water in place of milk	8 teaspoons cocoa powder dissolved in 2 tablespoons boiling water in place of milk

CHOCOLATE FUDGE ICING

This dark icing thickens as it cools, so if you get delayed and the icing has set too much to spread, beat in a little boiling water. This quantity will cover an 18 cm (7 inch) deep round or 15 cm (6 inch) deep square Small Madeira Cake (see page 12).

25 g (1 oz) butter

15 g (½ oz) cocoa powder

175 g (6 oz) icing sugar (no need to sift)

2 tablespoons milk

pinch of ground cinnamon (optional)

1 Melt the butter in a small saucepan over a low heat. Stir in the cocoa powder and cook over a medium heat, stirring constantly, for 30 seconds until smooth.

2 Remove from the heat and gradually stir in the sugar and milk, mixing until smooth. Mix in the ground cinnamon, if using.

3 Return to the heat and cook for 1 minute, stirring constantly, until the icing has a glossy pouring consistency. Quickly spread over the cake while the icing is still warm.

GLOSSY CHOCOLATE BUTTER ICING

A rich, dark, shiny icing made with a mixture of plain dark and milk chocolate so that it is full of flavour but without the bitterness of plain dark chocolate that children dislike. This quantity will cover a 23 cm (9 inch) deep round or 20 cm (8 inch) deep square Medium Madeira Cake (see page 13).

50 g (2 oz) butter

100 g (3½ oz) good-quality milk chocolate

100 g (3½ oz) good-quality plain dark chocolate

50 g (2 oz) icing sugar (no need to sift)

2 tablespoons milk

1 Melt the butter in a small saucepan over a low heat. Break the chocolate into pieces, add to the pan and heat gently, stirring occasionally, until just melted.

2 Remove from the heat and stir in the sugar and the milk. Return to the heat, if necessary, stirring constantly, until the icing is smooth and glossy. Use immediately.

Tip

As an alternative, this icing could be flavoured with a little finely grated orange rind or instant coffee powder.

DOUBLE CHOCOLATE GANACHE

A rich creamy icing made with warmed cream and half plain dark and half milk chocolate. It will set as it cools, so make it about 1 hour before you need it. This amount will cover an 18 cm (7 inch) deep round or 15 cm (6 inch) deep square Small Madeira Cake (see page 12). For a larger quantity, use 300 ml (½ pint) double cream and 300 g (10 oz) chocolate.

200 ml (7 fl oz) double cream

100 g (3½ oz) good-quality milk chocolate

100 g (3½ oz) good-quality plain dark chocolate

1 Heat the cream in a small saucepan over a medium heat until it is almost boiling and just beginning to bubble around the edges.

2 Remove the pan from the heat, break the chocolate into pieces and add to the pan. Set aside for 10 minutes or so, stirring occasionally, until the chocolate has melted.

3 Cover with clingfilm, leave to cool then chill in the refrigerator for 30 minutes–1 hour until thickened enough to hold its shape. The time will vary depending on how hot the cream was.

Tip

If you get delayed and the icing chills for longer – soften it once more by standing the basin in a saucepan of just boiled water for a minute or two. Stir before using.

WHITE CHOCOLATE CREAM

Deliciously chocolaty, this cream can be used to fill and cover an 18 cm (7 inch) deep round vanilla- or chocolate-flavoured Small Madeira Cake (see page 12) or a 23 cm (9 inch) deep round Medium Madeira Cake (see page 13), cut into 8 individual cakes using a 6 cm (2½ inch) plain biscuit cutter or upturned tumbler as a template using a small serrated knife, as for the White Chocolate Treats on page 93.

150 g (5 oz) white chocolate

300 ml (½ pint) double cream

1 Break the chocolate into pieces and put in a heatproof bowl set over a half-filled saucepan of just-boiled water. Set aside for 5 minutes, off the heat, until the chocolate has melted.

2 Whip the cream in a large bowl until it forms soft swirls. Stir the melted chocolate, then gently fold into the cream. Use immediately.

GLACÉ ICING

A quick-to-make, spoonable icing that can be used plain or coloured. If your child has adventurous tastes, try replacing the water with orange or lemon juice. This quantity will cover 12 Fairy Cakes (see page 16).

175 g (6 oz) icing sugar, sifted

3–4 teaspoons water

1 Sift the sugar into a medium bowl, pressing the last grains through the sieve with the back of a spoon.

2 Gradually stir in just enough of the measurement water to mix to a smooth thick icing that will flow from a spoon.

ROYAL ICING

Most often used to decorate wedding and Christmas cakes, here royal icing is also used to pipe on cake details or to stick icing decorations in place. Royal icing sets hard as it dries, so if making it in advance, cover the surface closely with clingfilm, stir before using and loosen the mixture with a few drops of lemon juice, if necessary.

1 dried egg white

225 g (7½ oz) icing sugar, sifted

1 Reconstitute the egg white with water according to the packet instructions.

2 Gradually whisk in the sugar a tablespoon or so at a time until the icing forms soft peaks that hold their shape. You may find that you do not need to add all the sugar.

Tip

Dried egg white is generally sold in small sachets that are the equivalent to two egg whites – make sure that you use only half a packet.

Techniques

The individual cake designs in this book detail the specific techniques involved in icing and decorating the cakes, but the following are the basic techniques that are routinely used.

USING READY-TO-ROLL ICING

Ready-to-roll icing may be sold plain white, in ivory or in a variety of pastel and vibrant colours ranging from pale lilac, pink and blue to cerise pink, turquoise, orange or purple and the deepest red or black. Whether you choose to buy white and colour your own with food colourings (see below) or buy ready coloured, the icing should be kneaded on a surface lightly dusted with a little sifted icing sugar to soften it slightly before rolling. Any icing that you are not going to use immediately must be tightly wrapped in a plastic bag or clingfilm so that it does not dry out.

FOOD COLOURINGS

These can be used to colour ready-to-roll icing, royal icing and butter icing, as well as desiccated coconut. They are most often sold in paste or liquid form and are very concentrated, so add them cautiously. For very intense, deep colours, opt for paste colourings. Reserve liquid colourings for creating pastel shades of icing, as the more of these you add, the stickier your icing can become, especially when using ready-to-roll icing. Add dots of colouring from the tip of a cocktail stick and gradually build up the colour until you achieve the desired shade, kneading well between additions. You can always add a little extra, but once added, the only way to reduce the colour is to mix with more icing. Sometimes a marbled effect is required. In this case, only partially mix in the colouring, then roll out for a colour-veined finish.

CHOOSING A CAKE BOARD

Traditionally, birthday cakes were always served on thick or thin foil-covered cake boards, but now with such a wide choice of coloured chinaware and other items and materials on offer, you may prefer to serve your cake on a china plate, a coloured wood, glass or a plastic chopping board.

COVERING A CAKE BOARD WITH READY-TO-ROLL ICING

1 Spread a little butter icing or jam thinly along the edge or edges of the cake board top.

2 Knead the ready-to-roll icing on a surface lightly dusted with sifted icing sugar until slightly softened. Lightly dust a rolling pin with icing sugar, then roll out the icing to a round or square a little larger (about 1 cm/½ inch) all around than the board, moving the icing and redusting the work surface lightly with icing sugar as needed.

3 Lift the icing on the rolling pin and drape it over the board. Smooth in place with your fingertips dusted with icing sugar.

4 Lift the board and trim off the excess icing around the edge or edges with a small knife.

5 Re-knead the icing trimmings, tightly wrap in a plastic bag or clingfilm and reserve.

Tip

For larger cake boards, you may find it easier to roll the icing straight on to the cake board lightly dusted with icing sugar with a rolling pin.

COVERING A CAKE WITH READY-TO-ROLL ICING

1 Put the cake on the cake board or plate and spread the top and side or sides thinly with butter icing or apricot jam.

2 Knead the ready-to-roll icing on a surface lightly dusted with sifted icing sugar. Lightly dust a rolling pin with icing sugar, then roll out the icing to a round or square about 12 cm (5 inches) larger in diameter than the cake top. Lift the icing on the rolling pin and drape over the cake.

3 Ease the icing over the sides of the cake, smoothing it with your fingertips dusted with icing sugar. As the icing is so pliable, you should be able to shape it without any creases.

4 Trim away the excess icing from the base of the board or plate with a small knife. Using the palms of your hands dusted with icing sugar, smooth out any bumps, making the surface as flat as you can.

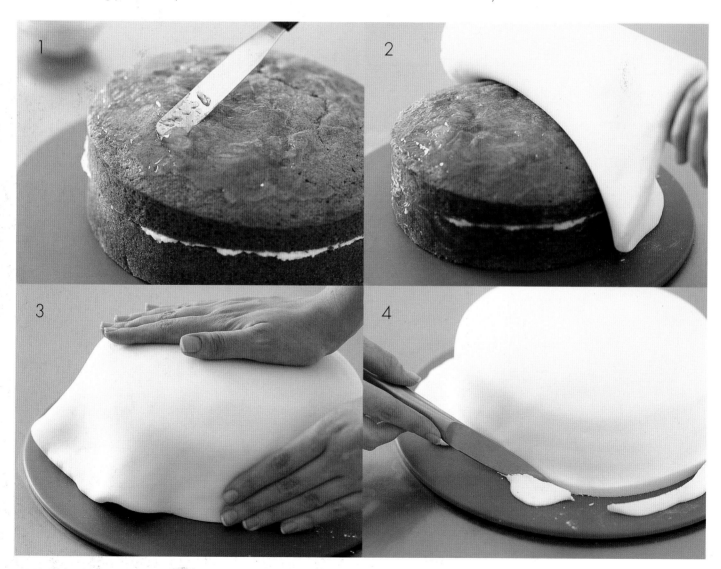

DECORATING A CAKE BOARD WITH AN ICING BORDER

Instead of covering a cake board with icing, you can add a border of icing to the cake board edge or edges once the cake has been decorated. Cut one long strip of rolled-out icing and join at the back of a round cake or cut strips the same length as the board sides of a square board and trim the ends diagonally so that the edges can be butted together neatly.

COVERING A CAKE WITH BUTTER ICING

1   Put the sandwiched cake on to a cake board or plate, then spread a little butter icing very thinly over the top and side or sides of the cake to stick the crumbs in place.

2   Spread a more generous layer of butter icing over the top and side or sides of the cake, smoothing in place with a small palette knife.

Finishing touches

This is the fun, creative part! But do not be nervous if you are a novice at cake icing. There are lots of inventive ways of using basic cut-out icing shapes, sweets and chocolates to add novelty and decorative details to your cakes with the minimum of time.

PIPED ICING

Tubes of ready-made icing with small detachable plastic piping tubes are sold in most supermarkets, as are smaller tubes of writing icing, which are ideal when only tiny amounts of piping are needed. Where larger amounts are required, you may prefer to use homemade royal icing (see page 25) and spoon it into a greaseproof paper piping bag. These are easy to make and you can simply snip off the tip to pipe the icing or use a piping tube.

CUTTING OUT ICING SHAPES

Stamping out shapes with cutters is a quick and easy way for even the most inexperienced at cake icing to decorate a cake. Cutters can be used to create hearts and stars, circles and triangles, numbers and flowers. Add the shapes immediately to the cake or leave to dry and prop up at angles on a dot of piped icing for an extra dimension.

Using plunger cutters offers a fail-safe way of stamping out tiny shapes, as the plunger gently pushes the icing shape out of the cutter easily every time.

Metal piping tubes can be used in a variety of ways to cut out shapes. The tips of large cream plain piping tubes, either 8 mm (⅜ inch), 5 mm (¼ inch) or 1 cm (½ inch), can be used to cut out small rounds as well as larger rounds using the upturned ends. Small piping tubes can be used to cut out tiny rounds, again using the upturned end.

To create crescent moon shapes, cut out rounds with biscuit cutters or piping tubes, then use the same cutter or tube to cut partially into each round to cut a crescent shape.

Shapes do not need to be solid. Try cutting a smaller shape from a larger one to make heart, star or circle frames, then leave empty or fill with a second coloured shape.

HOW TO MAKE A PIPING BAG

1 Cut a 25 cm (10 inch) square of greaseproof paper and fold in half to make a large triangle. Fold the triangle in half through the folded edge and pinch the second folded edge to mark the central fold.

2 Open out again. Holding the centre of the long folded edge towards you, curl the left-hand point of the triangle over to meet the centre pinch mark, forming a cone.

3 Next, bring the right-hand point over and around the cone so that the 3 points meet.

4 Lastly, fold the top points down several times to prevent the paper cone from unravelling.

TO USE THE BAG

Half-fill the bag with icing, fold the top edge down to enclose the icing, then snip off the tip. Make only a tiny snip, then squeeze out a little icing. Enlarge the hole with scissors if the piping needs to be larger. If using a metal piping tube, snip off the tip and drop the tube into the bag, enlarging the hole if needed so that it fits snugly with half the tube showing, then half-fill the bag with icing. For larger piping tubes, use a reusable fabric or plastic bag with a ready-cut tip.

MAKING FLOWERS

Specialist cake-icing shops sell a great range of fancy-shaped cutters, but you can easily be swept away with the choice. Try to go for shapes that you will use more than once, such as a set of different-sized flower plunger cutters or daisy cutters, rather than a single complicated orchid or rose.

To give added shape to flowers, press the flower out of the plunger cutter on to a piece of foam – a new foam washing-up sponge is ideal. This will curl the edges of the petals. Alternatively, curl the flowers on pieces of crumpled nonstick baking paper set in a bun tray. Once the flowers have been shaped, transfer them to a baking sheet lined with nonstick baking paper to harden.

If, when cutting flowers, the icing sticks to the cutter, then dip the cutter into a little icing sugar between use.

MAKING CHOCOLATE CURLS

These always look effective and are very simple to make, especially if the chocolate is at room temperature.

1 Turn a bar of chocolate over so that the smooth underside is uppermost. Position on the edge of a work surface.

2 Using a swivel-bladed vegetable peeler, pare away thin shavings of chocolate from the bar. If the curls are very small, warm the chocolate in a microwave oven for 10–15 seconds on High (if 650 watt) or Medium (if 700 watt) and try again.

3 For smaller, finer curls, grate the chocolate on to a plate instead using a medium or small grater setting.

WRAPPING CAKES WITH CHOCOLATE

This eye-catching but easy decoration is made by spreading melted chocolate on to a strip of nonstick baking paper that is a little taller than the side of your cake and long enough to wrap right around the outside of the cake. The secret is to melt the chocolate gently so that it stays glossy.

1 Bring a saucepan of water to the boil then set a large heatproof bowl over it so that it will heat up but not touch the water. Break the chocolate into the bowl, then remove the pan from the heat and leave for 5 minutes until the chocolate has melted.

2 Stir, then spread the chocolate over the strip of paper right up to one long edge and then make a wavy, jagged or swirly edge a little way down from the opposite long edge.

3 Press the chocolate on to the side of the cake so that the paper is on the outside, the soft chocolate is pressed against the cake and the decorative edge is uppermost.

4 Chill until set, then peel away the paper. Decorate the side of the cake with ribbon, if liked.

USING SWEETS AND CHOCOLATES

Adding brightly coloured sweets or chocolates to cakes creates maximum impact for minimum effort. These items can easily be used to give the effect of eyeballs (see page 36), spots (see page 90), jewels (see page 50), spider legs (see page 132), whiskers (see page 62) or simple lines of colour (see page 80).

USING CANDLES

For very young children, it just wouldn't be a birthday cake without a candle to mark each year of their age. Look out for pastel- or primary-coloured ones, dotty or glittery ones, shaped, wiggly or wand-like ones, numerical candles, those that spell 'happy birthday' or even those that will not blow out! Add candles to candleholders to catch the melting wax or make your own with tiny balls or shapes of ready-to-roll icing.

Tiny tots

Cheeky pirate

serves 10
decoration time 1 hour

double quantity Butter Icing (see page 21)

pink paste food colouring

Large round Quick-mix Sandwich Cake (see
   page 14)

23 cm (9 inch) thin round cake board or plate

250 g (8 oz) red ready-to-roll icing

sifted icing sugar, for dusting

75 g (3 oz) white ready-to-roll icing

1 round blue liquorice sweet

50 g (2 oz) royal blue ready-to-roll icing

25 g (1 oz) black ready-to-roll icing

1 gold foil-covered coin

Tip

The bandanna colours can be varied
according to the colours of icing that you
happen to have. For example, use a
combination of blue, green and white,
or green, yellow and brown.

1 Colour the butter icing pale pink with the colouring, then use
some of the icing to sandwich the cakes together. Put on to
the cake board or plate. Reserve 2 teaspoons of the butter
icing and spread the remainder over the top and side of the
cake, smoothing with a small palette knife.

2 Knead the red icing on a surface lightly dusted with icing
sugar until slightly softened. Roll out until a little larger than
half the cake top. Cut a straight edge with a knife. Drape the
icing over the cake so that the cut edge covers one-third of
the cake top in a diagonal line, draping downwards on the
right-hand side of the cake to the cake board, and add a
few pleats to resemble a bandanna. Trim off the excess.

3 Re-knead and roll out the trimmings. Cut out a mouth shape
and 2 very thin strips for the ends of the mouth and press in
place on the cake.

4 Knead and roll out the white icing. Cut out small rounds
using the upturned end of a piping tube and press these at
intervals on to the bandanna, sticking them in place with a
little water. Roll a small white icing ball, then flatten, shape
into an oval eye and press on to the pirate's face. Add the
blue sweet for the eyeball and stick in place with a tiny dot
of the reserved butter icing. Colour the remaining white icing
pale pink with the colouring and shape into an ear. Press on
to the side of the cake.

5 Knead and roll out the blue icing. Cut out more spots for the
bandanna. Knead and roll out the black icing. Cut out a
semicircle for an eyepatch. Shape the remaining black icing
into a thin rope and press above the eyepatch, across the
face and over the ear. Add a gold coin earring and stick in
place with a dot of butter icing.

King of the road

serves 20
decoration time 45 minutes

1 Trim the top of the cake level, if needed. Cut the cake horizontally in half, then sandwich back together with most of the butter icing. Put on to the cake board or plate. Spread the top and side very thinly with the remaining butter icing.

2 Cut off 200 g (7 oz) of the white icing, wrap and reserve. Knead the remaining icing, roll out and use to cover the top and sides of the cake and the cake board. Smooth with the fingertips, trim off the excess and wrap the trimmings.

3 Colour the 200 g (7 oz) reserved white icing pale grey with a little of the black colouring. Shape three-quarters of the grey into a long rope 46 cm (18 inches) long, then flatten it into a strip 3.5 cm (1½ inches) wide with a rolling pin. Straighten one long edge, then cut the opposite edge into a wavy line. Position around the lower side of the cake, wavy edge uppermost, sticking it in place with a little water, if necessary. Trim off the excess. Knead and roll out the reserved grey icing and cut out a winding road and stick on to the cake top with a little water. Colour the trimmings black, wrap and reserve.

4 Knead and roll out the red icing and cut out 2 cars 7 cm (3 inches) long. Knead and roll out the blue icing and cut out 2 lorries of similar size. Press on to the cake, leaving space for the yellow cars. Knead and roll out a little yellow icing, cut out 2 cars and press into the spaces. Roll small black balls then flatten for wheels. Press on to the cars, sticking in place with water.

5 Shape a larger 3-D car from the remaining yellow icing and position on the road, standing on pieces of icing trimmings, then cover these with black wheels. Roll out the white icing trimmings, cut out small shapes for car windows and add. Roll small balls and press on for headlights. Add tiny white strips for road markings. Cut very thin strips from any remaining red and black icing, trim and press on to the large yellow car bonnet and boot. Add lollipop road signs.

23 cm (9 inch) deep round Large Madeira Cake (see page 13)

one-and-a-half quantity Butter Icing (see page 21)

28 cm (11 inch) thin round cake board or plate

700 g (1 lb 7 oz) white ready-to-roll icing

sifted icing sugar, for dusting

black paste food colouring

75 g (3 oz) red ready-to-roll icing

75 g (3 oz) blue ready-to-roll icing

175 g (6 oz) yellow ready-to-roll icing

2 red lollipops, unwrapped

Tips

• For a child who may be getting a toy race track for a birthday present, use a little more grey icing and make it into a circular roadway on top of the cake.

• Use any remaining icing trimmings to make additional road signs by covering cocktail sticks with ropes of icing then adding flattened balls of coloured icing. Leave to dry flat on nonstick baking paper, then pipe on details – perhaps the child's age or name – with tubes of writing icing.

Magic numbers

serves 8
decoration time 45 minutes

8 cm (7 inch) deep round Small Madeira Cake
(see page 12)

single quantity Butter Icing (see page 21)

20 cm (8 inch) thin round cake board or plate

400 g (13 oz) white ready-to-roll icing

sifted icing sugar, for dusting

blue paste food colouring

125 g (4 oz) yellow ready-to-roll icing

125 g (4 oz) red ready-to-roll icing

125 g (4 oz) orange ready-to-roll icing

Tips

- Adjust the sum to relate to the age of the particular individual – this is a great cake for all ages, including bigger birthdays such as 18, 40 or even 80!
- Boxed sets of small number cutters can be bought from good cookware shops, cookware departments in large department stores or specialist cake-icing shops.

1 Cut the cake horizontally in half, then sandwich back together with most of the butter icing. Put on to the cake board or plate. Spread the top and side very thinly with the remaining butter icing.

2 Knead the white icing on a surface lightly dusted with icing sugar until slightly softened. Roll out and use to cover the cake. Smooth in place with your fingertips dusted with icing sugar, then trim off the excess.

3 Colour the trimmings bright blue with the food colouring and knead until an even colour. Wrap and reserve.

4 Knead and roll out a little of the yellow icing and cut out a number 2 and different-sized stars with small cutters. Knead and roll out some red icing and cut out a number 3 and some stars. Knead and roll out some of the orange icing and cut out some number 5s and some stars.

5 Arrange the yellow 2, the red 3 and one orange 5 on top of the cake, leaving spaces in between. Stick coloured stars randomly over the cake top with a little water.

6 Roll out the reserved blue icing, cut some small narrow strips and press on to the cake top between the numbers for plus and equals signs. Stamp out a few tiny stars and press on to the cake top, then cut out large stars from the remaining blue.

7 Stick the large blue stars around the side of the cake, leaving spaces in between for numbers. Add alternate-coloured 5s to the spaces, using the orange 5s you cut out earlier and re-kneading and rolling out the rest of the icing trimmings to cut 5s from other colours, as necessary.

Alien invasion

serves 6
decoration time 45 minutes

6 Muffins (see page 17) or bought large
  muffins, paper cases removed

single quantity vanilla-flavoured Butter Icing
  (see page 21)

selection of liquorice or fruit sweets

150 g (5 oz) bright pink ready-to-roll icing

sifted icing sugar, for dusting

large round plate

150 g (5 oz) blue ready-to-roll icing

150 g (5 oz) green ready-to-roll icing

2 black liquorice Catherine wheels

1 Stand the muffins on a chopping board and spread the butter
icing over the tops and sides to cover. Press on the liquorice
or fruit sweets for eyes and noses.

2 Knead the pink icing on a surface lightly dusted with icing
sugar until slightly softened. Roll out thinly and cut narrow
strips. Drape the strips randomly over the tops of 2 muffins so
that they cover the butter icing and extend down and over
the work surface. Carefully transfer to a large round plate.

3 Repeat with each of the remaining pieces of different-
coloured icing until each of the 6 muffins has been covered
with the different-coloured strips.

4 To complete, press pieces of unwound Catherine wheel into
the top of the muffins for antennae.

Tip

Let your imagination run riot and add
whacky coloured feet, mouths or ears
made out of icing or sweets.

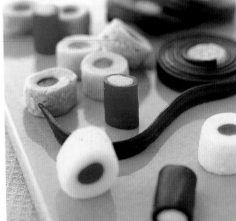

High flyer

serves 12
decoration time 1 hour

30 x 23 x 5 cm (12 x 9 x 2 inch) roasting tin
Medium Madeira Cake (see page 13)

one-and-a-half quantity Butter Icing
(see page 21)

25 x 35 cm (10 x 14 inch) rectangular cake
board, covered with 500 g (1 lb) pale blue
ready-to-roll icing, or similar-sized glass
chopping board

500 g (1 lb) white ready-to-roll icing

sifted icing sugar, for dusting

375 g (12 oz) red ready-to-roll icing

75 g (3 oz) grey ready-to-roll icing

2 black and white liquorice sweets, 1 halved,
1 quartered

Tips

- Although this design is for a young
child, the colours could be changed
and easily adapted to make a Spitfire,
Mosquito or other plane for a model-
making enthusiast. Borrow the kit box
for reference for the correct colours
and markings.
- If the liquorice sweets are too heavy to
stick, use the remaining butter icing from
the edge of the bowl as glue.

1 Put the cake top downwards on a chopping board with
a narrow edge nearest you. Cut a 12.5 cm (5 inch) strip
the length of the longest side for the plane body. Cut the
remaining piece in half through the longest edge. Reserve
one piece for wings. Cut a 2 cm (¾ inch) strip off the side of
the remaining piece. Reserve for the top tail fin. Put the last
piece on to the plane body and shape into the cockpit,
rounding off the front, tapering the back and sides and
sloping the roof. Curve the edges of the plane.

2 Cut the reserved wing cake horizontally in half to form
2 thinner wings. Shape the tips and cut a slim diagonal slice
off the other side to butt against the body of the plane.

3 Stick all the plane body parts together with butter icing,
keeping the wings and tail fin separate. Spread the outside
thinly with butter icing, then the wings and tail fin. Lift the
body on to the cake or chopping board to sit diagonally.

4 Knead and roll out the white icing to 33 x 23 cm (13 x 9
inches), drape over the cake and smooth in place. Trim off the
excess. Re-knead, roll out and cover the top tail fin. Cut the side
tail detail from the icing trimmings and stick in place with water.

5 Knead and roll out one-third of the red icing and cut 2 strips
30 x 2.5 cm (12 x 1 inch) then press around the base of the
plane, butting up to the side tail detail and front nose cone.
Cut a curved strip for the nose cone and stick in place. Use
the remaining red icing to cover the wings. Butt them against
the plane body. Cut the top tail fin details from the trimmings.

6 Knead and roll out the grey icing and cut a semicircle for the
front window and round side windows and stick in place. Cut
strips for the wing and fin details. Stick 2 sweet quarters in
front of each wing and a halved sweet to each side of the tail.

space ship

serves 10
decoration time 1 hour

1 Cut the sandwich cake horizontally in half. Level the basin cake top, if necessary, then cut horizontally in half. Sandwich both cakes back together with some of the butter icing. Spread the top of the sandwich cake with some of the butter icing and put the basin cake, trimmed top downwards, on top.

2 Transfer the cake stack to the smaller cake board and spread the remaining butter icing thinly all over the top and sides.

3 Knead the white icing on a surface lightly dusted with icing sugar until slightly softened. Roll out to a 30 cm (12 inch) round. Lift over the cake with a rolling pin, smooth in place and trim off the excess. Stand the cake stack on a saucer or lid on the icing-covered larger cake board or plate so that it is raised slightly above it.

4 Reknead and roll out the icing trimmings. Cut out tiny stars with a mini cutter. Cut out rounds in 2 sizes using the upturned end of a small- and medium-sized piping tube, then cut part way through the larger rounds to create crescent moon shapes. Add the flying saucer sweets to the board or plate, reserving one.

5 Stick the round blue liquorice sweets and white chocolate buttons alternately around the side of the bottom cake with piped dots of royal or writing icing.

6 Stick the green twisted bootlaces around the base of the top cake with piped dots of icing. Stick candy-covered chocolate drops above, adding 2 blue, then a green. Stick jelly sweets in a line above, adding 2 orange, then a green.

7 Decorate the top of the space ship with lollipops. Add the reserved flying saucer, with the square liquorice sweet and an offcut of bootlace, cut side uppermost, on top, securing with piped dots of royal or writing icing.

Large single Quick-mix sandwich cake (see page 14) and 900 ml (1½ pint) pudding basin Medium Madeira Cake (see page 13)

one-and-a-half-quantity Butter Icing (see page 21)

20 cm (8 inch) thin round cake board

500 g (1 lb) white ready-to-roll icing

sifted icing sugar, for dusting

saucer or jam jar lid

30 cm (12 inch) thin round cake board, covered with 375 g (12 oz) deep blue ready-to-roll icing, or a large blue plate

flying saucer sherbet sweets

14 round blue and 1 square orange liquorice sweets

14 white chocolate rainbow buttons

2 tablespoons Royal Icing (see page 25) or 1 tube white writing icing

4 green apple-flavoured twisted bootlaces, cut to short lengths

20 blue and 11 green candy-covered chocolate drops

7 mixed lime green, yellow and orange lollipops

18 orange and 10 green jelly sweets

Tip
Vary the sweets according to your child's particular preferences. Look out for fruity versions of liquorice sweets too.

Knight's castle

serves 24
decoration time 1 hour

20 cm (8 inch) deep square chocolate-flavoured
Large Madeira Cake (see page 13)

one-and-a-half quantity chocolate-flavoured
Butter Icing (see page 21)

25 cm (10 inch) thin square cake board, covered
with 200 g (7 oz) black ready-to-roll icing, or
plate

1 kg (2 lb) white ready-to-roll icing

sifted icing sugar, for dusting

black paste food colouring

28 cm (11 inch) chocolate-flavoured Swiss Roll
(see page 18) or 23 cm (9 inch) bought
chocolate Swiss roll

400 g (13 oz) deep blue ready-to-roll icing

little Royal Icing (see page 25), coloured grey

little Royal Icing (see page 25), coloured black or
tube black writing icing

4 chocolate sticks

25 g (1 oz) yellow ready-to-roll icing

25 g (1 oz) green ready-to-roll icing

Tips

- If you are short of time, then use bought
  cocktail stick flags for the pennants on
  the turret tops.
- If you choose to bake your own Swiss roll
  for this cake from the recipe on page 18
  you will find you have quite a bit to spare
  after making the turrets and gate tower.
  This can be eaten as a cook's perk!

1 Trim the top of the cake level, if needed. Cut the cake horizontally in half and sandwich back together with some of the butter icing. Reserve 4 tablespoons of the butter icing and spread the remainder thinly over the top and sides. Place on the cake board or plate.

2 Knead the white icing, then colour grey with the black colouring until partially mixed and mottled.

3 Wrap and reserve 150 g (5 oz) of the grey icing. Use the remainder to cover the cake. Trim off the excess and reserve.

4 Cut the Swiss roll into four 5 cm (2 inch) thick slices for turrets and one 2.5 cm (1 inch) thick slice. Cut the latter in half and use one half for the gate tower. Spread the top and sides of the Swiss roll pieces with most of the remaining butter icing.

5 Roll out the remaining grey icing in batches. Cut four 6 cm (2½ inch) plain rounds with a biscuit cutter and press on to the turret tops. Cut four 5 x 23 cm (2 x 9 inch) pieces and cover the turret sides. Cover the gate tower with a smaller piece. Reserve any trimmings. Stick the Swiss roll pieces in place with the last of the butter icing.

6 Knead and shape half the blue icing into a rope 1.5 cm (¾ inch) thick. Cut into 1.5 cm (¾ inch) wide slices and cut every other one in half. Stick these alternate-sized 'bricks' around the fort top and the turret tops with a little piped grey royal icing. Repeat until all the top edges are covered. Cut a blue door from the trimmings. Stick on to the fort front.

7 Colour the remaining grey ready-to-roll icing black. Roll out, cut large and smaller squares. Stick around the door and corners of the castle with grey piped icing. Pipe on a black portcullis. Press chocolate sticks into the turrets. Roll out the yellow and green ready-to-roll icing, cut flags and attach.

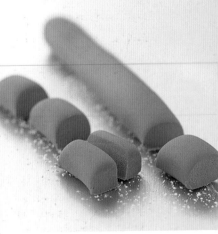

Fairy princess crowns

serves 12
decoration time 45 minutes, plus drying

single quantity Butter Icing (see page 21)

pink paste food colouring

12 Fairy Cakes (see page 16) or bought fairy
cakes, paper cases removed

500 g (1 lb) pale pink ready-to-roll icing

sifted icing sugar, for dusting

mauve sugar sprinkles

blue and pink icing shapes

red jelly diamonds

1 tube fine white or pink writing icing or little
Royal Icing (see page 25)

large round or square plate

1 Colour the butter icing pale pink with the food colouring.
Trim the tops of cakes level, if needed, then turn each cake
top downwards and spread the butter icing over the new
tops and sides.

2 Knead the pink ready-to-roll icing on a surface lightly
dusted with icing sugar until slightly softened. Roll out one-
third and cut 3 strips 20 x 5 cm (8 x 2 inches) long. Using
the upturned end of a large cream plain piping tube, cut a
scalloped edge along one of the long edges. Repeat on
the other 2 icing strips.

3 Press an icing strip, scalloped edge uppermost, around one
cake to form a crown, trimming off the excess and reserving.
Press the tips of the crown upright – if they are very floppy,
trim a little off the tips. Use the trimmings to make a fourth
crown then continue with the remaining icing. Repeat until all
12 crowns have been made.

4 Spoon the mauve sprinkles inside each crown, then decorate
the sides with icing shapes and jelly diamonds, sticking them
in place with dots of piped writing or royal icing. Transfer the
crowns to a plate. Leave for 30 minutes in a cool place for
the icing to harden.

Tip
Look out for tubs of different-coloured
sprinkles and tiny sugar decorations.
Each tub is divided into five or six sections,
each containing a toning sprinkle or icing
sugar decoration.

Daisy chain

serves 10
decoration time 1 hour, plus drying

Large round Quick-mix Sandwich Cake (see page 14)

single quantity Butter Icing (see page 21)

25 cm (10 inch) thin round cake board, covered with 375 g (12 oz) white ready-to-roll icing, or plate

500 g (1 lb) pale yellow ready-to-roll icing

sifted icing sugar, for dusting

white vegetable fat, for greasing

50 g (2 oz) white flower paste (see tip, below)

3 tablespoons Royal Icing (see page 25), coloured pale green

1 tablespoon Royal Icing (see page 25), coloured yellow, or 1 tube yellow writing icing

1 metre (39 inches) x 2 cm (¾ inch) wide pale green chiffon ribbon

Tips

- Make sure that you bake the cakes in straight-sided rather than sloping tins for a smooth-sided finish.
- Flower paste can be bought from specialist cake-icing shops and can be rolled very much more thinly than ordinary ready-to-roll icing.

1 Sandwich the cakes together with some of the butter icing. Transfer to the cake board or plate. Reserve 1 teaspoon of the butter icing and spread the remainder thinly over the top and side of the cake.

2 Knead the yellow ready-to-roll icing on a surface lightly dusted with icing sugar until slightly softened. Roll out and use to cover the cake. Smooth the top and side with your fingers dusted with icing sugar. Trim off the excess.

3 To make the flowers, rub a little vegetable fat over a chopping board, rolling pin and base of a 2.5 cm (1 inch) and 2 cm (¾ inch) plastic daisy cutter. Cut off half the flower paste, wrap and reserve. Roll out the remaining flower paste thinly. Stamp out a few flower shapes at a time and lift off the board with a small knife on to pieces of crumpled nonstick baking paper to shape. Leave to dry for 30 minutes. Continue stamping, re-kneading and rolling out the trimmings, and using the reserved flower paste, until it has all been used up.

4 Spoon the pale green royal icing into a greaseproof paper piping bag (see page 31), snip off the tip and pipe a swirly line over the top and slightly over the side of the cake for a daisy stem. Stick the flowers at intervals over the piped stem, adding some to the base of the cake board with dots of green piped icing.

5 Pipe dots of yellow icing in the centres of the flowers. Tie the ribbon in a bow around the side of the cake and trim off the excess ribbon.

Sunflower cup cakes

serves 12
decoration time 30 minutes

1 Trim the tops of the fairy cakes level, if needed. Divide the butter icing between the tops of the cakes then spread into an even layer.

2 Knead the yellow icing on a surface lightly dusted with icing sugar until slightly softened. Roll out and cut into 2.5 cm (1 inch) wide strips. Cut each strip into triangular-shaped petals and stick around the edge of each cake.

3 Add a second row of icing petals, a little in from the first, re-rolling the trimmings as needed. Knead and roll out the brown icing and cut out 2.5 cm (1 inch) circles with a fluted cutter. Press into the centre of each flower.

4 Pipe on red mouths and black eyes with writing icing. Arrange the cakes on the plate.

single quantity Butter Icing (see page 21)

12 Fairy Cakes (see page 16), with green foil paper cases

250 g (8 oz) yellow ready-to-roll icing

sifted icing sugar, for dusting

125 g (4 oz) brown ready-to-roll icing

1 tube red writing icing

1 tube black writing icing

large green plate

Tip
Chocolate sweets or jumbo chocolate buttons could be used for the flower faces, if preferred.

Mini birthday cakes

serves 12
decoration time 20 minutes, plus drying

single quantity Glacé Icing (see page 24)

mauve paste food colouring

pink or red paste food colouring

yellow paste food colouring

12 Fairy Cakes (see page 16), with white
 paper cases, or bought fairy cakes

4 each of yellow and white, pink, mauve and
 white candles

75 g (3 oz) dolly mixture sweets

75 g (3 oz) candy-covered chocolate drops

large round or square plate

1 Put one-third of the glacé icing into a separate bowl and colour lilac with a little mauve colouring. Spoon half the remaining icing into another bowl and colour pale pink with the pink colouring or with a little of the red colouring. Colour the remaining icing pale yellow.

2 Spoon the yellow icing over 4 of the fairy cakes, the lilac icing over another 4 and the pink icing over the remaining cakes, smoothing in place with the back of the spoon.

3 Add a yellow and white candle to the centre of each yellow iced cake, then press co-ordinating-coloured sweets around the base of each candle. Repeat with the correspondingly coloured candles and sweets for the remaining cakes. Transfer the cakes to a plate. Leave in a cool place for the icing to set for 30 minutes before serving.

Tip

For chocolate fans, cover chocolate-flavoured fairy cakes with Chocolate Fudge Icing (see page 22), brightly-coloured sweets and candy-covered chocolate drops.

Flying Kite

serves 20
decoration time 45 minutes

double quantity Butter Icing (see page 21)

blue paste food colouring

23 cm (9 inch) deep round Large Madeira
    Cake (see page 13)

25 cm (10 inch) thick round cake board `
    or plate

125 g (4 oz) white ready-to-roll icing

sifted icing sugar, for dusting

75 g (3 oz) deep blue ready-to-roll icing

75 g (3 oz) deep pink ready-to-roll icing

small piece red ready-to-roll icing or 1 tube red
    writing icing

Tip

Instead of a kite, draw an aeroplane on a
piece of greaseproof paper, then cut off
the wings. Roll out different colours for the
body and wings and press on the cake,
perhaps with a birthday banner tied to the
back of the plane.

1 Colour the butter icing pale blue with the colouring. Trim the top of the cake level, if needed. Cut the cake horizontally in half and sandwich back together with some of the butter icing. Put the cake on to the cake board or plate and spread the remaining butter icing over the top and side, smoothing it with the back of a palette knife.

2 Knead and roll out the white icing on a surface lightly dusted with icing sugar. Cut out cloud shapes with a knife. Press over the top and side of the cake. Wrap the trimmings.

3 Cut a kite template from a piece of greaseproof paper or nonstick baking paper about 10 cm (4 inches) along the top 2 edges and 13 cm (5¼ inches) along the lower 2 edges. Fold vertically in half to form 2 larger triangles and horizontally across the points to form 2 smaller triangles. Cut along the fold lines to separate the triangles.

4 Knead and roll out the deep blue icing and, using the kite template, cut out one smaller triangle from one side of the kite and one larger from the opposite side. Repeat with the deep pink icing. Press the triangles on to the cake top so that the kite tip overlaps the edge of the cake slightly. (If the kite tip begins to droop, prop it up with a rolled ball of foil and remove just before serving the cake.)

5 Shape most of the remaining blue icing into a long string and drape under the kite and over the edge of the cake. Cut out tiny triangles of pink icing and arrange in pairs for bows along the blue string.

6 Shape the reserved white icing into 2 oval eyes and press on to the kite, adding eyeballs shaped from the remaining blue icing. Shape the red icing into a mouth and press on to the kite, or pipe on a mouth with writing icing, if preferred.

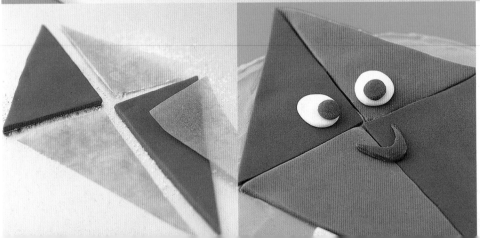

Noughts and crosses

serves 9
decoration time 20 minutes, plus drying

150 g (5 oz) red ready-to-roll icing

sifted icing sugar, for dusting

150 g (5 oz) yellow ready-to-roll icing

9 Fairy Cakes (see page 16) or bought
   fairy cakes

single quantity Butter Icing (see page 21)

20 cm (12 inch) square plate or thin cake
   board

7 wide strawberry-flavoured jelly strips

1 Make a cross template by cutting a rectangle 6 x 5 cm (2½ x 2 inches) from paper or cardboard, then cut out a small triangle from the centre of each long side and a larger triangle from each of the short sides.

2 Knead the red icing on a surface lightly dusted with icing sugar until slightly softened. Roll out and cut around the template to make 5 crosses. Put on to a baking sheet lined with nonstick baking paper lightly dusted with icing sugar.

3 Knead and roll out the yellow icing and cut out 4 rounds with a 5 cm (2 inch) plain biscuit cutter. Stamp out a small circle from the centre of each round using the tip of a large cream piping tube or an upturned icing piping tube. Add to the baking sheet and leave to dry for at least 1 hour.

4 Spread the butter icing over the centre of the fairy cakes and top with the dried icing shapes. Arrange on the plate or cake board with a grid made from the jelly strips, cut into appropriate lengths and overlapped as shown.

Tip

This idea could easily be adapted to make a crossword with stamped-out letters on a larger jelly-strip grid.

Magician's hat

serves 16
decoration time 1 hour

1 Trim the tops of the chocolate cakes level, if needed, then sandwich them together with some of the butter icing. Spread a little of the remaining butter icing over the side, filling in any gaps where the cakes join. Put on to the icing-covered cake board or plate.

2 Knead the black icing on a surface lightly dusted with icing sugar until slightly softened. Roll out and cut a strip 55 x 15 cm (22 x 6 inches) or long and tall enough to go around the side of the cake stack. Carefully lift the icing and press on to the cake stack side. Trim off the excess, wrap and reserve.

3 Spread the uncovered cake board with a little butter icing. Knead and roll out the grey icing and use to cover the top of the board. Roll out the reserved black icing into a strip 73 x 3.5 cm (29 x 1½ inches) and press on to the edge of the board for the hat rim, trimming off the excess. Stick the cake board on to the cake stack top with some butter icing.

4 For the rabbit, cover the muffin with butter icing and stick in place on the cake top with butter icing. Cut a thin diagonal slice off each sponge roll and position on the cake for ears and paws, securing the ears with cocktail sticks for extra support, if necessary. Spread these with butter icing.

5 Knead and roll out the pink icing, cut out ear and paw pads and press in place. Form a U-shaped mouth and press in place.

6 Add dolly mixture eyes and nose, pressing liquorice bootlace whiskers under the nose. Stick rainbow pearl eyeballs to the eyes with a little butter icing. Knead and roll out the white icing, cut out large and small stars and stick to the hat with the remaining butter icing. Leave the icing to harden for a few hours before serving.

2 x 18 cm (7 inch) deep round chocolate-flavoured Small Madeira Cakes (see page 12)

double quantity Butter Icing (see page 21)

23 cm (9 inch) thin round cake board, covered with 375 g (12 oz) mauve ready-to-roll icing, or coloured plate

625 g (1¼ lb) black ready-to-roll icing

sifted icing sugar, for dusting

125 g (4 oz) grey ready-to-roll icing

23 cm (9 inch) thin round cake board

1 muffin (see page 17) or bought muffin, paper case removed

4 bought mini chocolate, jam or vanilla sponge rolls

50 g (2 oz) pink ready-to-roll icing

1 round dolly mixture sweet, halved

1 pink square dolly mixture sweet

small piece black liquorice bootlace, snipped into short lengths

2 pink rainbow pearls

75 g (3 oz) white ready-to-roll icing

Tip

Short of time? Then use three 30 cm (6 inch) shop-bought chocolate sandwich cakes and a bought muffin and roll out black icing to fit the height and circumference of the cake stack.

Bunch of balloons

serves 8
decoration time 45 minutes

18 cm (7 inch) deep round Small Madeira
    Cake (see page 12)

single quantity Butter Icing (see page 21)

20 cm (8 inch) thin round cake board or plate

400 g (13 oz) orange ready-to-roll icing

sifted icing sugar, for dusting

25 g (1 oz) red ready-to-roll icing

25 g (1 oz) deep blue ready-to-roll icing

25 g (1 oz) yellow ready-to-roll icing

75 g (3 oz) white ready-to-roll icing

selection of different-coloured narrow ribbons

1   Trim the top of the cake, if needed, then cut the cake horizontally in half and sandwich back together with some of the butter icing. Put on to the cake board or plate. Reserve 2 teaspoons of the butter icing and spread the remainder thinly over the top and side.

2   Knead the orange icing on a surface lightly dusted with icing sugar until slightly softened. Roll out and use to cover the cake, smoothing in place with your fingertips dusted with icing sugar. Trim off the excess, wrap and reserve.

3   Knead and roll out the red icing, cut out 2 balloon shapes and arrange on the cake top, with a piece of ribbon, about 15 cm (6 inches) long, tucked under each balloon. Repeat with the blue and yellow, then make one balloon with the white icing. Tie the balloon ribbons together with another ribbon, then trim the ends diagonally with scissors.

4   Shape the remaining white icing into a rope about 58 cm (23 inches) long. Repeat with the reserved orange icing, then twist the ropes together and press on to the base of the cake board, sticking in place with the reserved butter icing.

Tip

Vary the colours of the balloons and cake to suit your child's favourite colours. You might also like to pipe on your child's name, piping a letter on to each balloon.

Sweet-guzzling monster

serves 20
decoration time 50 minutes, plus drying

1.5 litre (2½ pint) pudding basin Medium Madeira Cake (see page 13)

18 cm (7 inch) deep round Small Madeira Cake (see page 12)

one-and-a-half quantity Butter Icing (see page 21)

25 cm (10 inch) thick round silver cake board or plate

750 g (1½ lb) white ready-to-roll icing

sifted icing sugar, for dusting

green paste food colouring

100 g (3½ oz) pale pink ready-to-roll icing

125 g (4 oz) purple ready-to-roll icing

15 g (½ oz) white ready-to-roll icing

selection of sweets and lollipops

Tip
To make a spooky Halloween version, cover the cake in white icing and add ghoulish black lips, eyeballs and eyebrows.

1 Level the basin cake top, if needed. Cut each cake horizontally in half and sandwich back together with butter icing. Spread the top of the round cake with butter icing, then transfer to the cake board or plate, positioning the cake slightly off-centre close to the side of the cake board. Press the basin cake, trimmed top downwards, on top.

2 Reserve 2 teaspoons of the butter icing and spread the rest over the cake top and sides.

3 Knead the white icing on a surface lightly dusted with icing sugar until slightly softened. Knead in a little green colouring until partially mixed and faintly marbled. Roll out into a 35 cm (14 inch) round. Lift on the rolling pin and drape over the cake so that it falls in folds, easing it down to the board with your fingertips, if necessary. Leave space between the front folds for the mouth.

4 Knead and roll out the pink icing thickly. Cut out 2 feet and tuck under the front of the green icing. Roll out the icing a little thinner and cut out an oval-shaped mouth 10 x 7 cm (4 x 3 inches). Stick in place with a little water. Reserve trimmings for hands.

5 Knead and roll out one-third of the purple icing into a rope 12 cm (5 inches) long for the top lip, pinch together in 2 places, then stick on to the mouth with a little of the reserved butter icing. Cut out an oval 12 x 7 cm (5 x 3 inches) from the remaining purple icing, dot the lower underside edges with butter icing and stick on to the mouth to create a pouch.

6 Shape the purple icing trimmings into 2 arched eyebrows and 2 eyeballs. Shape the white icing into 2 eyes. Stick the features in place with water or butter icing. Cut out hands from the reserved pink icing and stick to the front of the cake. Leave to dry for at least 30 minutes, then add sweets to the mouth.

Older kids

Grand master

serves 20
decoration time 1 hour

20 cm (8 inch) deep square Large Madeira
    Cake (see page 13)

one-and-a-half quantity Butter Icing
    (see page 21)

23 cm (9 inch) thin square cake board or plate

1 kg (2 lb) white ready-to-roll icing

sifted icing sugar, for dusting

125 g (4 oz) dark blue ready-to-roll icing

125 g (4 oz) black ready-to-roll icing

1.25 metres (49 inches) x 2.5 cm (1 inch) wide
    blue and white checked ribbon

1 Level the top of the cake, if needed. Cut the cake horizontally in half and sandwich back together with some of the butter icing. Put on to the cake board or plate and spread the remaining butter icing thinly over the top and sides.

2 Cut off 125 g (4 oz) of the white icing, wrap and reserve. Knead the remainder on a surface lightly dusted with icing sugar until slightly softened. Roll out and use to cover the top and sides of the cake, smoothing in place with your fingertips dusted with icing sugar. Trim off the excess and add to the reserved white icing.

3 Knead and roll out the blue icing thinly to 10 x 20 cm (4 x 8 inches). Cut vertically into eight 2.5 cm (1 inch) wide strips, then cut horizontally into 4 equal-sized strips to make 32 squares. Arrange these on top of the cake in a chequerboard pattern with 4 in each row.

4 Make stylized chess pieces from the reserved white icing and the black icing based on different-sized triangles of icing, adding tiny flattened balls of icing and rounded balls of different sizes for the pawns, bishop, king and queen. Make a diagonal cut in the top of the bishop. Add different-shaped crowns to the king and queen and tiny castellated strips to the rook or castle. For the knight, add an oval head and cut a small strip with one side cut into a thin fringe for the mane. Add ears and stand on a small plinth.

5 Arrange the chess pieces on the cake to look as if a game is in progress, with a few pieces beside the cake board. Tie the ribbon around the side of the cake.

Tip

As the chess pieces are relatively time-consuming to make, don't attempt to make a full set, but give the impression that a game is halfway through, with some of the pieces already taken.

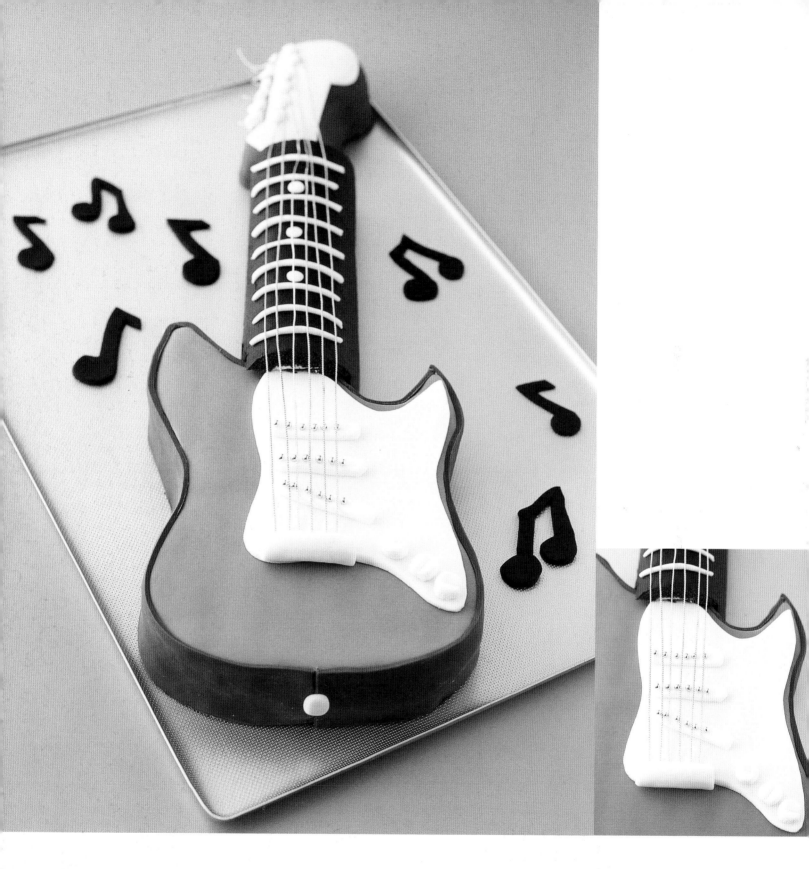

Rock fan

serves 12
decoration time 1 hour

1 Put the roasting tin cake, base uppermost, on to a large chopping board with the Swiss roll butted up against one of the short edges. Trim the large cake to resemble a guitar body (see picture opposite). Cut a guitar head from the cake trimmings.

2 Cut the guitar shape horizontally in half and sandwich back together with some of the butter icing. Transfer to the cake board or tray, leaving space for the guitar 'neck'. Spread the top and sides thinly with more butter icing and spread the rest over the head.

3 Knead the coffee-coloured icing, roll out and use to cover the top of the guitar. Trim off the excess. Knead and roll out three-quarters of the dark brown icing and cut two strips each 23 x 5 cm (9 x 2 inches). Press around the sides of the guitar, butting the edges together at the top and bottom. Roll out and cover the head with the remainder. Add the Swiss roll neck and the shaped head to the cake board or tray.

4 Knead and roll out the white icing. Cut out a rectangle 18 x 12 cm (7 x 5 inches), then shape as in the picture. Press on to the guitar body. Cut 3 small string rests and 3 volume control knobs from the trimmings and press on. Cut a piece for the top of the head. Shape small balls of icing for string tighteners. Stick in place.

5 Roll out thin ropes of white icing and stick on to the Swiss roll at intervals, adding flattened balls of icing in between with piped white icing. Pipe dots of icing over the string rests and add 6 silver balls to each.

6 Tie lengths of silver cord around the string tighteners and secure on the guitar with balls of icing. Snip off the excess and cover with a thick rectangular strip of white icing. Knead, roll out and cut black musical icing notes to decorate the board or tray.

30 x 23 x 5 cm (12 x 9 x 2 inch) roasting tin chocolate-flavoured Medium Madeira Cake (see page 13)

28 cm (11 inch) chocolate-flavoured Swiss Roll (see page 18) or 28 cm (11 inch) bought chocolate Swiss roll

single quantity chocolate-flavoured Butter Icing (see page 21)

62 x 25 cm (25 x 10 inch) thin silver cake board or larger coloured tray

375 g (12 oz) coffee-coloured ready-to-roll icing

sifted icing sugar, for dusting

375 g (12 oz) dark brown ready-to-roll icing

250 g (8 oz) white ready-to-roll icing

2 tablespoons Royal Icing (see page 25)

18 edible silver balls

4 metres (13 feet) fine silver cord

125 g (4 oz) black ready-to-roll icing

Tips

- The cake or chopping board required is such an unusual size that you may prefer to serve the cake on a large plastic tray instead and cover it with foil or coloured foil wrapping paper.
- If you find that the cord for the guitar strings keeps unravelling, secure it around a halved cocktail stick, then cover this with icing, but make sure to remove it before cutting the cake.

Soccer star

serves 10
decoration time 1 hour

2 x 900 ml (1½ pint) pudding basin Medium
Madeira Cakes (see page 13)

single quantity Butter Icing (see page 21)

500 g (1 lb) white ready-to-roll icing

sifted icing sugar, for dusting

23 cm (9 inch) thin cake board or round plate

125 g (4 oz) black ready-to-roll icing

100 g (3½ oz) blue ready-to-roll icing (or
colour of your child's favourite team)

1 tube coloured writing icing (optional)

Tips

- Roll out extra icing for the hexagons as
necessary, keeping the remainder well
wrapped to prevent it from drying out
and making shaping difficult.
- The top of a spice jar makes an ideal
circle template for the first stage of
making the hexagon template.
- If using a cake board, you may like
to cover it with green butter icing or
green-coloured desiccated coconut to
resemble grass.

1 Level the basin cake tops, if necessary, and sandwich
together with some of the butter icing to form a ball shape.
Reserve 1 tablespoon of the remaining butter icing and
spread the remainder thinly over the outside of the cake.

2 Knead and roll out two-thirds of the white icing thinly. Use to
cover the cake, smoothing with your fingertips dusted with
icing sugar. Trim off the excess, wrap and reserve. Transfer
the cake to the cake board or plate.

3 Create a hexagon template by cutting a 3.5 cm (1½ inch)
round from greaseproof paper. Fold the round in half, then
fold the half into 3. Cut a straight line between the ends of
the fold lines, then open out.

4 Knead and roll out a little of the black icing and cut out a
black hexagon. Press on to the cake top. Roll out a little of
the reserved white trimmings and cut out white hexagons,
arrange these around the black one and press or nudge the
shapes so that they fit exactly. Add a row of black hexagons,
then more white hexagons, sticking in place down the sides
of the ball with dots of the reserved butter icing. As you cover
more of the cake, you may need to trim down the hexagon
shapes slightly to fit. Reserve a little white icing.

5 Knead and roll out the blue icing and cut out 3 rounds of
decreasing size with fluted biscuit cutters, the largest 7 cm
(3 inches). Frill the edges by rolling a cocktail stick back and
forth over them. Press one on top of the other for the rosette.
Add a small round of the reserved white icing to the centre.
Cut strips of the blue icing for the rosette tails. Arrange the
rosette by the side of the football. Pipe your child's name or
age on to the centre of the rosette, if liked.

speedy skater

serves 6
decoration time 45 minutes

4 chocolate-covered marshmallow teacakes

28 cm (11 inch) chocolate-flavoured Swiss Roll (see page 18) or 28 cm (11 inch) bought chocolate Swiss roll

25 cm (10 inch) thin square cake board, covered with 250 g (8 oz) white or mauve ready-to-roll icing, or mauve plate

2 tablespoons apricot jam

single quantity Chocolate Fudge Icing (see page 22)

100 g (3½ oz) yellow ready-to-roll icing

sifted icing sugar, for dusting

75 g (3 oz) black ready-to-roll icing

250 g (8 oz) grey ready-to-roll icing

Tips

- If you are planning to give some skates as a birthday present, then adapt the colours on the cake to match them.
- If you are putting the cake on an icing-covered board, you may find it easier to spread the Swiss roll with fudge icing before you move it to the cake board.
- For a smooth finish to the chocolate fudge icing, use a small palette knife dipped into boiling water when smoothing it.

1 Put the teacakes on to a chopping board and position the Swiss roll just above so that the left-hand side aligns with the first teacake. Cut the Swiss roll at an angle on the right-hand side, just behind the last teacake, for the boot heel. Put the trimming at right angles to the first piece to form the boot leg.

2 Shape the boot toe and put the trimming at the top of the boot leg to add extra height to the skate. Transfer all of the cakes to the cake board or plate. Spread the cut edges of the Swiss roll with jam.

3 Spread the fudge icing over the top and sides of the Swiss roll and smooth with a knife.

4 Knead the yellow icing on a surface lightly dusted with icing sugar until slightly softened. Roll out and cut a strip 18 x 10 cm (7 x 4 inches). Press on to the inside top of the boot leg for a lining tongue. Knead and roll out the black icing, cut a strip and press next to the yellow for the boot lining.

5 Knead and roll out two thirds of the grey icing and cut out a curved shape for the boot leg reinforcement. Drape over the boot leg and smooth in place. Cut a strip 12 x 1.5 cm (5 x ¾ inch), mark with knife cuts, then press on to the boot leg for an adjustable strap. Make a small black clip with grey detail.

6 Roll out the remaining grey icing, cut a strip 20 x 5 cm (8 x 2 inches) and shape to make a wheel guard. Press halfway over the wheels and halfway over the boot base.

7 Cut 2 more strips for boot straps from the grey trimmings, press in place and add clips as in Step 5. Roll out the remaining black icing thinly, cut thin strips and squares and press on to the boot for moulding detail. Roll small balls of yellow and grey, flatten and stick to the wheels and leg reinforcement with water for rivets.

Crashed skier

serves 8
decoration time 50 minutes, plus drying

50 g (2 oz) grey ready-to-roll icing

sifted icing sugar, for dusting

75 g (3 oz) black ready-to-roll icing

cocktail sticks

50 g (2 oz) red ready-to-roll icing

15 g (½ oz) pale pink ready-to-roll icing

1.2 litre (2 pint) pudding basin Small Madeira
    Cake (see page 12)

double quantity Butter Icing (see page 21)

20 cm (8 inch) thin square cake board or plate

4 tablespoons desiccated coconut

little black paste food colouring

Tips

- Remove the body and cocktail sticks before slicing the cake.
- If you are very short of time, use a washed child's action doll, cut the cake vertically in half and sandwich back together with the doll in the middle, or if using a broken doll, leave the cake whole. Put the clothes back on the doll once the cake has been iced.

1 Roll out the grey icing thickly and cut 2 skis 12 x 1 cm (5 x ½ inch). Round one end of each ski and curl up slightly. Shape 2 thin ropes 10 cm (4 inches) long for poles, taper one end of each, then wrap a thin rope around a little way from the tapered end. Leave to harden on a baking sheet lined with nonstick baking paper for 3 hours, or overnight.

2 Roll out the black icing thickly and cut 2 trouser legs 7 x 1 cm (3 x ½ inch). Stick a cocktail stick into one end of each so that it extends about 2.5 cm (1 inch). Stick grey ski boots to the other end with water. Leave to partially dry with the skis. Reserve the trimmings.

3 For the skier's arms and trunk, shape most of the red icing into a semicircle with a 6 cm (2½ inch) long base. Cut 2 cuts up from the base 1 cm (½ inch) in from either side but not all the way through and shape into outstretched arms. Shape the pink icing into a head with a small nose, adding a tiny skewer hole for the mouth. Add a black hat with red icing detail and attach to the shoulders with a cocktail stick. Shape a black scarf and gloves and add to the skier. Add 2 more cocktail sticks to the waist. Leave to dry.

4 Level the cake top, if needed. Cut horizontally in half and sandwich back together with a little butter icing. Put the cake, trimmed top downwards, on to the cake board or plate.

5 Reserve 1 tablespoon of the butter icing and spread the remainder over the top and side of the cake, and a little over the board or plate.

6 Press the body into the top of the cake and the legs halfway down. Spread a little butter icing over the trousers and body. Sprinkle the cake and skier with coconut. Attach skis to ski boots and poles to gloves. Paint on eyes with black colouring.

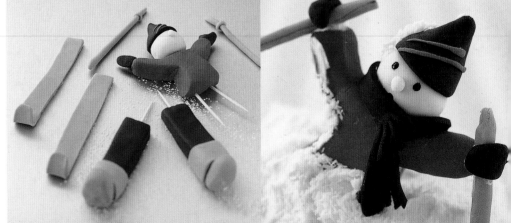

Chocolate extravaganza

serves 20
decoration time 30 minutes, plus drying

20 cm (8 inch) deep square chocolate-
flavoured Large Madeira Cake
(see page 13)

single quantity Glossy Chocolate Butter Icing
(see page 22)

25 cm (10 inch) thick square cake board
or plate

165 g (5½ oz) bag white chocolate-covered
malt balls

165 g (5½ oz) bag milk chocolate-covered
malt balls

1 Level the top of the cake, if needed. Cut the cake horizontally
in half and sandwich back together with a little of the icing.

2 Put the cake on a wire rack set over a baking sheet and pour
the remaining icing on to the cake top. Gently spread over
the top and down the sides with a small palette knife,
scooping up the icing from the baking sheet to fill in any
gaps at the base of the cake.

3 Carefully transfer the cake to the cake board or plate.
Arrange alternate-coloured malt balls in diagonal rows over
the top of the cake, with a single row around the base of the
cake. Leave to set in a cool place for at least 30 minutes
before serving.

Tip

Vary the sweets on top of the cake
according to your child's preference or
make the cake multicoloured by adding
a variety of sweets in different colours.

Hearts and flowers

serves 14–16
decoration time 30 minutes

1 Put the cake on to a chopping board and level the top, if needed. Make a greaseproof paper heart template by drawing around the cake board and cutting out the heart. Trim a little off all the way around the template edge until it fits the cake top. Cut the cake around the heart template.

2 Cut the cake horizontally in half and sandwich back together with some of the butter icing. Transfer to the cake board. Spread the remaining butter icing over the top and side of the cake.

3 Lightly knead the pale pink icing on a surface lightly dusted with icing sugar until slightly softened. Roll out until a little larger than the cake. Lift on a rolling pin and drape over the cake, then smooth in place with your fingertips dusted with icing sugar. Trim off the excess.

4 Re-knead the trimmings and roll out. Cut out flower and heart shapes of different sizes using plunger cutters, pressing them out on to a piece of foam sponge so that they curl (see page 32), then transfer to a baking sheet lined with nonstick baking paper dusted with a little icing sugar. Make dark pink or red and white flowers and hearts in the same way from the remaining ready-to-roll icing.

5 Arrange the flowers and hearts over the cake top and stick in place with tiny dots of piping icing or piped royal icing. Add dots of icing to the centre of some of the larger flowers and add candles. Tie the ribbon around the side of the cake and decorate the cake board with extra flowers and hearts.

23 cm (9 inch) deep round Large Madeira Cake (see page 13)

24 cm (9½ inch) thin heart-shaped cake board

one-and-a-half quantity Butter Icing (see page 21)

625 g (1¼ lb) pale pink ready-to-roll icing

sifted icing sugar, for dusting

75 g (3 oz) deep pink or red ready-to-roll icing

75 g (3 oz) white ready-to-roll icing

1 tube white piping icing or 2 tablespoons Royal Icing (see page 25)

pale pink candles

1 metre (39 inches) x 2.5 cm (1 inch) wide pink ribbon

Tip

For a St. Valentine's Day version, use a chocolate-flavoured cake and cover it with a single quantity of Glossy Chocolate Butter Icing (see page 22) and add red and pink hearts of varying size.

Rugby scrum

serves 14–16
decoration time 1¼ hours

1 Level the top of the cake, if needed. Trim off and round the corners to make an hour-glass shape, then slope the opposite sides of the cake slightly for the players to lean against.

2 Cut the cake horizontally in half and sandwich back together with butter icing. Put the cake on to the cake board or plate. Spread butter icing thinly over the top and sides and roughly on the board or plate to resemble a muddy pitch.

3 Knead the green (or favourite team's colour) icing on a surface lightly dusted with icing sugar until slightly softened. Divide into 10 pieces. Reserve 2 pieces for socks and roll each of the remaining pieces into a 6 cm (2½ inch) square. Make a small cut on either side of each square in from the bottom corner and almost to the top of the square, then shape into arms and a body. Arrange one row of 3 shirts facing the centre of the cake, with arms stretched over the next player's shoulders. Knead and roll out the white icing and add a row of rectangular white shorts with a small slit in the base of each. Add a second row of 4 shirts and shorts a little back from the first, with the shirts curving over the edge of the cake. Add the eighth man to the centre of the side of the cake. Repeat for the team on the other side of the scrum.

4 Knead the pink icing and shape a head for each player on the edge of the scrum and one or two extra heads with button noses and small holes for mouths. Shape hands for the players.

5 Shape short pink sausage shapes for thighs and same-sized pieces from the teams' coloured icing reserved in Step 3 for socks. Add black oval pieces for boots. Shape a rugby ball from the remaining black icing and trim with white icing.

6 Pipe on black hair and facial features. Pipe white numbers on to the shirt backs and studs on some boots.

20 cm (8 inch) deep square chocolate-flavoured Large Madeira Cake (see page 13)

one-and-a-half quantity chocolate-flavoured Butter Icing (see page 21)

33 cm (13 inch) thin round cake board or plate

375 g (12 oz) green ready-to-roll icing (or favourite team's colour)

sifted icing sugar, for dusting

375 g (12 oz) red ready-to-roll icing (or opponent team's colour)

250 g (8 oz) white ready-to-roll icing

250 g (8 oz) pink ready-to-roll icing

150 g (5 oz) black ready-to-roll icing

1 tablespoon Royal Icing (see page 25), coloured black, or 1 tube black writing icing

2 tablespoons white Royal Icing (see page 25) or 1 tube white writing icing

Tip

Modify the shirts, socks and numbers to adapt this cake for American football and create ready-to-roll icing helmets and shoulder pads for the players. Choose colours to match your favourite teams.

Funky boots

serves 10
decoration time 1 hour, plus drying

2 x 28 cm (11 inch) chocolate-flavoured Swiss
Rolls (see page 18) or 2 x 28 cm (11 inch)
bought chocolate Swiss rolls

3 tablespoons raspberry jam

4–6 long wooden satay sticks

500 g (1 lb) mauve ready-to-roll icing

sifted icing sugar, for dusting

18 cm (7 inch) square cake board or plate

125 g (4 oz) pale pink ready-to-roll icing

200 g (7 oz) deep pink ready-to-roll icing

Tips

• If the boots seem a little wobbly, stand a
tall sauce bottle or bag of flour behind
each boot leg before leaving to dry. The
boots are best iced the day before they
are needed.

• Make sure you remove the satay sticks
before serving the cake to guests.

1 Cut each Swiss roll in half. Put two Swiss roll halves a little
apart on a chopping board for the boot feet. Stand a second
half of Swiss roll on top of one at one end for the boot leg
and secure with jam and satay sticks. Repeat to make a
second boot leg. Shape the boot feet by trimming away a
little of the cake.

2 Spread the cakes thinly with the remaining jam. Cut the
mauve icing in half, wrap one half and reserve. Knead the
remaining half on a surface lightly dusted with icing sugar
until slightly softened. Roll out thinly and drape over one of
the boots so that any joins will fall on the inside face of the
boot. Smooth in place with your fingertips dusted with icing
sugar. Trim off the excess. Fill any gaps with trimmings. Cover
the second boot in the same way. Carefully transfer to the
cake board or plate.

3 Knead and roll out the pale pink icing. Cut out two 6 cm
(2½ inch) rounds with a plain biscuit cutter and press on to the
top of the boot legs. Reserve the trimmings.

4 Knead and roll out the deep pink icing. Cut long strips 1 cm
(½ inch) wide. Press one around the top of each boot and a
second around the base of each boot, sticking in place with
a little water, and trim off the excess.

5 Cut heart shapes from re-rolled icing trimmings using
3 different-sized small cutters, then cut smaller shapes from
the 2 larger ones. Stick in place with water. Leave for at least
1 hour for the icing to harden.

Handbag heaven

serves 14–16
decoration time 50 minutes

20 cm (8 inch) deep square Large Madeira
  Cake (see page 13)

one-and-a-half quantity Butter Icing
  (see page 21)

36 x 25 cm (14 x 10 inch) rectangular cake
  board or large plate

750 g (1½ lb) pale pink ready-to-roll icing

sifted icing sugar, for dusting

150 g (5 oz) white ready-to-roll icing

250 g (8 oz) pale green ready-to-roll icing

6 pink sugar flowers

Tip

For an adult version, use a favourite
handbag as a guide and copy colours,
clasp and handle detail.

1   Put the cake on to a chopping board and level the top, if
    needed. Cut a thin curved slice from the top 2 opposite sides
    of the cake to about one-third down the length of the cake.
    To do so, turn the first piece of trimmed cake over and use it as
    a template to cut the second side. Slope the top edge of the
    handbag down towards the narrow side so that the edge
    where the handbag flap will go is shallower.

2   Cut the cake horizontally in half and sandwich back together
    with two-thirds of the butter icing. Put on to the cake board or
    plate. Reserve 2 teaspoons of the butter icing and spread the
    remainder thinly over the top and sides of the cake.

3   Knead the pink icing on a surface lightly dusted with icing
    sugar until slightly softened. Roll out thinly and use to cover
    the cake, smoothing with your fingertips dusted with icing
    sugar. Trim off the excess, wrap and reserve.

4   Knead the white icing, roll out thickly and cut out the top
    flap of the handbag. Press in place, smoothing with your
    fingertips. Reserve the trimmings.

5   Knead and roll out the pale green icing. Cut long strips 1 cm
    (½ inch) wide and stick as stripes on to the lower part of the
    bag with water, butting up against the flap and leaving space
    in between so the pink icing can be seen. Trim off the excess.

6   Cut a rectangle of pink icing 4 x 1 cm (1½ x ½ inch) and press
    on to the flap for a clasp. Cut a smaller green rectangle and
    add at right angles to the pink. Cut a white strip for a buckle.
    Stick flowers on to the flap with the reserved butter icing.

7   Roll the remaining pink, white and green icing into small balls
    and arrange alternate colours as a strap on the cake board,
    butting up to the handbag top.

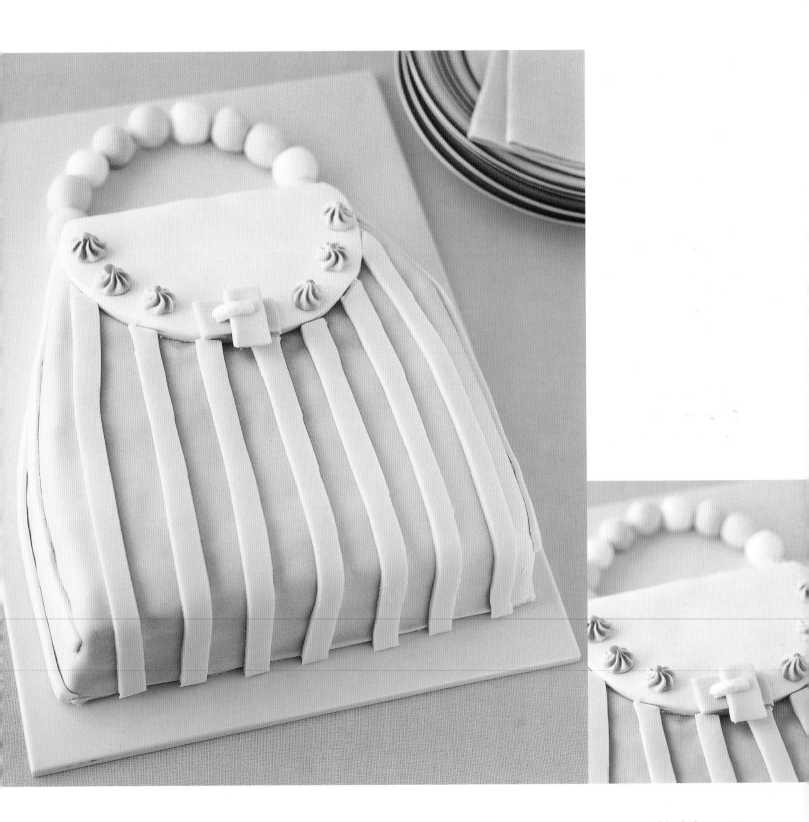

Chocolate bliss

serves 6
decoration time 45 minutes, plus drying

Shallow Cake (see page 17)

single quantity vanilla-flavoured Butter Icing
(see page 21)

25 cm (10 inch) round cake board, covered
with 200 g (7 oz) deep pink ready-to-roll
icing, or plate

900 ml (1½ pint) pudding basin Medium
Madeira Cake, made with half the 4-egg
mixture (see page 13)

625 g (1¼ lb) turquoise-blue ready-to-roll icing

sifted icing sugar, for dusting

cocktail sticks

40 g (1½ oz) milk or plain dark chocolate

1–2 teaspoons milk

few large marshmallows

100 g (3½ oz) bag candy-covered chocolate
drops

2 tablespoons Royal Icing (see page 25) or
1 tube writing icing

Tips

• Make sure you remove the cocktail sticks
  before serving the cake to guests.
• Coloured spots, hearts or flowers could
  be cut from coloured ready-to-roll icing
  as an alternative to the sweets spots on
  the cup and saucer.

1 Spread the top and sides of the shallow cake thinly with butter icing and put on a chopping board. Level the basin cake top, if needed, then place, trimmed top downwards, on to a chopping board. Cut horizontally in half and sandwich back together with some of the butter icing. Spread a little more of the butter icing thinly over the outside of the basin cake.

2 Knead the turquoise-blue icing on a surface lightly dusted with icing sugar until slightly softened. Cut off 150 g (5 oz) and wrap and reserve the remainder. Roll out the measured icing and use to cover the shallow cake, smoothing the surface with your fingertips dusted with icing sugar. Trim off the excess. Transfer to the cake board or plate.

3 Roll out the remaining blue icing and drape over the basin cake. Smooth over the surface, then carefully turn up the other way to resemble a cup. Trim off the excess and smooth the top edge. Put on to the shallow cake.

4 Re-knead the trimmings, roll into a thick rope 12 x 1 cm (5 x ½ inch) and shape into a cup handle. Press on to the cup side and secure with cocktail sticks. Prop up with pieces of crumpled foil.

5 Put the chocolate in a heatproof bowl and melt over a saucepan half-filled with gently simmering water. Stir into the remaining butter icing, mixing in enough milk to make a smooth glossy icing. Spread over the top of the cup and add the marshmallows to the centre.

6 Stick the coloured sweets over the cup and saucer with piped dots of royal or writing icing. Leave to harden for at least 1 hour. Remove the foil from under the cup handle before serving.

White chocolate treats

serves 8
decoration time 45 minutes, plus chilling

1 Trim the top of the cake level then, using a 6 cm (2½ inch) plain biscuit cutter or upturned tumbler as a template, cut out 8 smaller rounds of cake from the large cake using a small serrated knife. Cut each cake horizontally in half.

2 Add a spoonful of the white chocolate cream to 8 cake halves, then top with the remaining cake halves. Spread some white chocolate cream thickly over the top of each cake and then thinly around the sides.

3 Put the white chocolate in a heatproof bowl set over a saucepan half-filled with just-boiled water. Set aside for 5 minutes or so, off the heat, until the chocolate has melted. Cut 8 strips of nonstick baking paper 20 x 8.5 cm (8 x 3½ inches). Stir the chocolate, then spread over one strip right up to one long edge and then make a wavy swirled edge a little way down from the opposite long edge. With the wavy edge uppermost, press the strip of paper so that the chocolate touches the cream-spread edge of the cake and stands a little above the top. Smooth in place and repeat until all the cakes have been wrapped in the same way. Chill for 2 hours or until set.

4 Carefully peel the paper away from the chocolate, top the cakes with foil-wrapped sweets and decorate the sides of the cakes with ribbon. Transfer to a plate or cake board. Chill in the refrigerator until ready to serve.

23 cm (9 inch) deep round Large Madeira Cake (see page 13)

single quantity White Chocolate Cream (see page 24)

250 g (8 oz) white chocolate, broken into pieces

400 g (13 oz) foil-wrapped sweets

selection of thick and thin jewel-coloured ribbons in 3 colours, such as purple, pale pink and cerise pink

large round or square plate or cake board

Tips

- A plain dark chocolate version could be created in the same way, with small strawberries added to the tops of the cakes instead of the sweets.
- The cake trimmings may be used for a trifle or could be eaten as a cook's perk!

Flowers and butterflies

serves 8
decoration time 1 hour, plus chilling/drying

50 g (2 oz) white chocolate, broken into pieces

50 g (2 oz) plain dark chocolate

125 g (4 oz) pale pink ready-to-roll icing

sifted icing sugar, for dusting

18 cm (7 inch) deep round chocolate-flavoured
Small Madeira Cake (see page 12)

single quantity Double Chocolate Ganache
(see page 23)

23 cm (9 inch) pale pink cake board or plate

Tip

If the butterflies seem a little soft when you
take them out of the refrigerator, freeze
them for 10 minutes. You may find it helpful
to prop up the wings with some of the tiny
pink flowers.

1 Put the white chocolate in a heatproof bowl set over a
saucepan half-filled with just-boiled water. Set aside for
5 minutes or so, off the heat, until the chocolate has melted.
Stir, then spoon into a nonstick baking paper piping bag and
snip off the tip (see page 31). Pipe pairs of butterfly wings, in
the shape of a capital 'B' with its mirrored reflection for the
other wing, on to a baking sheet lined with nonstick baking
paper. Fill in the centres with squiggly piped lines and pipe
separate bodies, if liked.

2 Melt the plain dark chocolate in a separate bowl and use to
pipe butterflies as before. Chill the decorations in the
refrigerator for 45 minutes or until firm.

3 Meanwhile, knead the pale pink icing on a surface lightly
dusted with icing sugar until slightly softened. Roll out and
stamp out flower shapes with 4 different-sized biscuit cutters
ranging from 3 to 7 cm (1¼ to 3 inches) and some tiny
flowers with plunger cutters. Curl the petals by pressing into
sections of a bun tray lined with crumpled nonstick baking
paper (see page 32). Leave to dry for 30 minutes.

4 Cut the cake horizontally in half and sandwich back together
with some of the ganache. Transfer to the plate or cake
board. Reserve 1 tablespoon of the ganache and spread the
remainder over the top and side of the cake, smoothing with
a small palette knife.

5 Arrange the flowers over the top of the cake, with a few
around the base of the cake. Carefully lift the butterfly wings
off the paper and arrange in the flowers with dots of piped
ganache, then add the bodies to the butterflies, if using. Add
pale pink flower candles in between the flower and butterfly
icing decorations, if liked.

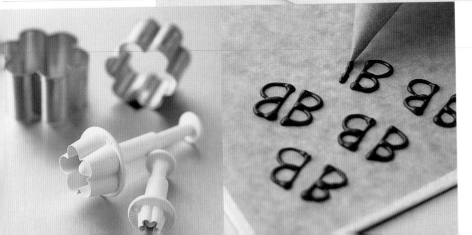

Bowled over

serves 12
decoration time 45 minutes

30 x 23 x 5 cm (12 x 9 x 2 inch) roasting tin
  Medium Madeira Cake (see page 13)

one-and-a-half quantity Butter Icing
  (see page 21)

33 x 25 cm (13 x 10 inch) rectangular cake
  board, covered with 375 g (12 oz) royal
  blue ready-to-roll icing, or plate

750 g (1½ lb) white ready-to-roll icing

sifted icing sugar, for dusting

200 g (7 oz) black ready-to-roll icing

75 g (3 oz) orange ready-to-roll icing

50 g (2 oz) turquoise ready-to-roll icing

Tip

If your child is a member of a bowling
club, then match the markings on the
skittles with those at the bowling alley.

1 Put the roasting tin cake on a chopping board so that the short edges are facing you. Cut a little off the top left- and right-hand sides to resemble the necks of 3 skittles, standing close together. Shape the bottom short edge into 3 curves for the skittle bases.

2 Cut the trimmed cake horizontally in half and sandwich back together with some butter icing. Put on to the cake board or plate and spread the top and sides thinly with the butter icing.

3 Cut off 250 g (8 oz) of the white icing, wrap and reserve. Knead the remaining icing on a surface lightly dusted with icing sugar until slightly softened. Roll out and use to cover the cake, smoothing in place with your fingertips dusted with icing sugar. Trim off the excess.

4 Re-knead one-third of the icing trimmings, roll out and cut into a tall skittle shape, the height of the cake and about one-third the width. Press on to the left-hand side of the cake top.

5 Knead and roll out the remaining white icing and cut out 2 more skittle shapes. Add one to the right-hand side of the cake, then press the third in the centre.

6 Knead and roll out the black icing. Cut out thin strips and use to edge the sides of the skittle markings and decorate the top. Stick in place with a little water. Reserve the trimmings.

7 Knead and roll out the orange icing. Cut out small rectangles and 3 narrow strips. Use to decorate the skittles. Knead and roll out the turquoise icing and cut into a 10 cm (4 inch) circle. Position on top of the skittles for the ball. Roll out the reserved black trimmings, cut out a number for the age of the birthday child, then press on to the ball.

Riding champ

serves 8–10
decoration time 1 hour

1 Level the cake top, if necessary. Turn the cake over, trimmed top downwards, cut into 3 horizontal layers and sandwich together with butter icing. Reserve 2 teaspoons of the butter icing and spread the remainder thinly over the top and side of the cake. Spread the reserved butter icing over half the cake board.

2 Knead the black icing on a surface lightly dusted with icing sugar until slightly softened. Cut off 50 g (2 oz) and wrap. Roll out the remainder until it covers half the cake board. Drape over the butter-iced end of the cake board for the hat peak and smooth with your fingertips dusted with icing sugar. Trim off the excess. Re-knead the trimmings and roll out. Cut out 2 ribbons for the back of the hat and 2 small buttons. Transfer to a sheet of nonstick baking paper.

3 Put the cake on to the cake board so that it almost touches the un-iced end and slightly covers the black 'hat peak' end.

4 Draw a triangular template for the coloured silks on nonstick baking paper with a base 11 cm (4½ inches) long and a height of 15 cm (6 inches). Cut out.

5 Knead the pale pink icing, roll out and use the template to cut out 3 triangular shapes. Press lightly on to the cake, leaving spaces in between. Cut out 3 deep pink triangles and press into the gaps, readjusting the position of the triangles slightly as necessary, trimming away the excess or pressing the edges together so that the cake is neatly covered. Smooth with your fingertips dusted with icing sugar.

6 Put the cake board on to a plate and place the black ribbons at the back. Roll out the reserved black icing and cut a strip 51 x 2 cm (21 x ¾ inches). Stick around the base of the hat with a little water. Add a black button to back and top.

1.5 litre (2½ pint) pudding basin Medium Madeira Cake (see page 13)

single quantity Butter Icing (see page 21)

23 x 18 cm (9 x 7 inch) thin oval cake board or plate

250 g (8 oz) black ready-to-roll icing

sifted icing sugar, for dusting

250 g (8 oz) pale pink ready-to-roll icing

250 g (8 oz) deep pink ready-to-roll icing

Tip
You may like to add a ribbon or icing rosette to finish off the cake, with the age of your child or a birthday message piped or written on to the centre. See page 74 for details of how to make a rosette from ready-to-roll icing.

Ice cream dream

serves 12
decoration time 50 minutes

30 x 23 x 5 cm (12 x 9 x 2 inch) roasting tin
   chocolate-flavoured Medium Madeira Cake
   (see page 13)

double quantity vanilla-flavoured Butter Icing
   (see page 21)

35 x 25 cm (14 x 10 inch) rectangular cake
   board, covered with 375 g (12 oz) lilac
   ready-to-roll icing, or plate

500 g (1 lb) pale yellow ready-to-roll icing

4 chocolate-flavoured Muffins (see page 17)
   or large bought muffins

pink or red paste food colouring

green paste food colouring

brown paste food colouring

1 To make the cone, cut the roasting tin cake into a triangle 18 x 23 cm (7 x 9 inches) on a chopping board. The trimmings are not needed (see Tip).

2 Cut the cone horizontally in half and sandwich back together with some butter icing. Spread the top and sides thinly with butter icing. Transfer the cone to the cake board or plate.

3 Knead the yellow ready-to-roll icing on a surface lightly dusted with icing sugar until slightly softened. Roll out two thirds, drape over the cone to completely cover and smooth in place. Trim off the excess and knead with the remaining icing. Roll out and use to cover the left half of the cone. Smooth in place and trim off the excess. Mark the icing with criss-cross lines to resemble wafer biscuit.

4 Trim a vertical slice off 2 of the muffins, then butt against the cone, with a third muffin above them. Trim a slice off the base of the remaining muffin and set aside.

5 Divide the butter icing into four portions, leaving one plain. Colour the second pink, the third pale green and the remaining portion light brown. Spread each colour over a different muffin and arrange as ice cream scoops, with the trimmed edges butted next to the cone.

Tip

To make use of the cake trimmings, split and sandwich them together with extra butter icing, spreading some on top too. Cut into small shapes and decorate with sweets. Alternatively, use the sponge as the base for a trifle or tiramisu.

Gifts galore

serves 28
decoration time 1 ¼ hours

1 Level the cake tops, if needed. Cut each cake horizontally in half and sandwich back together with butter icing. Put the square cake on to the cake board and spread the top and sides thinly with a little butter icing. Reserve 1 tablespoon of the butter icing and spread the remainder over the other 2 cakes. Put these cakes aside.

2 Cut off one-quarter of the burgundy icing, wrap and reserve. Knead the remaining icing on a surface lightly dusted with icing sugar until slightly softened. Roll out and use to cover the square cake, smoothing in place with your fingertips dusted with icing sugar. Trim off the excess and reserve.

3 Cut off one-third of the white icing, wrap and reserve. Use the remainder to cover the larger round cake. Trim off the excess and reserve. Put on top of the square cake.

4 Cut off one-quarter of the blue icing, wrap and reserve. Use the remainder to cover the small round cake. Trim off the excess and reserve. Put on top of the other cakes.

5 Roll out the reserved blue icing and cut 4 strips 9 x 2.5 cm (3½ x 1 inch). Stick to the sides of the base cake with butter icing, to resemble ribbons. Trim the tops of the strips where they butt up against the round cake. Reserve the trimmings.

6 Make burgundy ribbon strips for the centre cake and white strips for the top cake in the same way. Cut an extra strip of white and form into 2 loops for a bow, adding 2 smaller strips for the ribbon ends.

7 Roll out the remaining blue icing trimmings and cut tiny rounds with the upturned end of a piping tube. Stick over the centre cake with a little water. Cover the top of the cake board with a strip of white icing (see page 29). Stick the ribbon on to the side of the cake board with sticky tape.

20 cm (8 inch) deep square Large Madeira Cake (see page 13)

1 x Small Madeira Cake mixture (see page 12) split between 1 x 15 cm (6 inch) deep round tin and 1 x 9 cm (3½ inch) small baked bean can (see Tips), baked

double quantity Butter Icing (see page 21)

25 cm (10 inch) thick square cake board

750 g (1½ lb) burgundy ready-to-roll icing

sifted icing sugar, for dusting

500 g (1 lb) white ready-to-roll icing

250 g (8 oz) pale blue ready-to-roll icing

1 metre (39 inches) x 1 cm (½ inch) narrow white ribbon

double-sided sticky tape

Tips

- Use a 200 g (7 oz) baked bean can for the tiny cake.
- Remove the top and bottom of the baked bean can before use, wash well and peel away the label. Stand it on a baking sheet and line with nonstick or greaseproof paper as if lining the base and sides of a larger tin (see page 11).

Animal magic

My little kitten

serves 10
decoration time 30 minutes

2 small sandwich cakes (see page 15), each
    filled with 2 tablespoons jam, or 2 bought
    filled vanilla or chocolate sandwich cakes

30 x 25 cm (12 x 10 inch) oval cake board or
    large plate

double quantity Butter Icing (see page 21)

red and yellow or orange food colouring

2 jumbo green candy-coated chocolate beans

2 standard brown candy-coated chocolate
    beans

6 chocolate sticks

125 g (4 oz) orange ready-to-roll icing

sifted icing sugar, for dusting

1 Put one cake on to the cake board or plate for the body then prop the second up against it for the cat's head.

2 Spoon one third of the butter icing into a separate bowl and colour it orange.

3 Spread the head and body with the remaining uncoloured butter icing, then spoon on some orange butter icing to create the effect of ginger markings, easing it into stripes and swirls with the tip of a small knife.

4 Press the green sweetie eyes in position, then stick on brown sweetie eyeballs with a little butter icing. Break a little off the end of the chocolate sticks and press into the cake for whiskers. Knead the orange ready-to-roll icing on a surface dusted with a little icing sugar. Shape a small ball into a nose shape, then use more icing to create two triangular ears, four round paws and a thin rope for the mouth. Mark the paws with a knife and add to the cake.

Tip

If the cake is very crumbly, spread it with a little jam before topping with the butter icing so that the crumbs are stuck in place.

Puppy love

serves 10
decoration time 1 hour, plus drying

1.2 litre (2 pint) and 750 ml (1¼ pint)
   pudding basin Medium Madeira Cakes
   (see page 13)

25 cm (10 inch) thin round cake board or plate

double quantity vanilla-flavoured Butter Icing
   (see page 21)

cocktail sticks

4 bought mini jam sponge rolls

200 g (7oz) bar white chocolate

15 g (½ oz) white ready-to-roll icing

sifted icing sugar, for dusting

40 g (1½ oz) black ready-to-roll icing

15 g (½ oz) red ready-to-roll icing

125 g (4 oz) pale yellow ready-to-roll icing

Tip
Make sure you remove the cocktail sticks
before serving the cake to guests.

1 Level the basin cake tops, if necessary. Put the larger one, trimmed top downwards, on to the cake board or plate for the dog's body. Spread the outside with a little butter icing. Put the smaller cake on top, trimmed top downwards, slightly off centre for the head, and secure with butter icing and cocktail sticks.

2 Scoop out eye sockets in the top cake with a teaspoon and shape a small muzzle. Stick 2 sponge roll front legs at the front of the cake with a little butter icing and the remaining 2 towards the back for back legs.

3 Reserve 3 teaspoons of the butter icing and spread the remainder all over the cake to cover completely.

4 Run a swivel-bladed vegetable peeler over the smooth underside of the chocolate bar to create curls (see page 32). Stick the curls all over the dog with a round-bladed knife.

5 Roll small balls of white icing for the eyes, flatten into ovals and press in place. Add tiny balls of black icing for eyeballs and stick in place with dots of butter icing. Shape the remaining black icing into a round nose and stick on to the muzzle. Mark with the end of a cocktail stick. Shape the red icing into a curved tongue and add to the face.

6 Roll out two-thirds of the yellow icing thickly and cut out floppy ears. Stick in place with a little of the reserved butter icing, propping them up with pieces of crumpled foil or nonstick baking paper. Roll a ball of yellow icing, cut in half and make 3 small cuts in each half. Add to the front legs for paws. Shape 2 larger back paws from short sausage shapes and add cuts as before. Shape the remaining icing into a tail and press in place. Leave for at least 30 minutes for the ears to harden, then remove the foil or paper before serving.

Cute teddy

serves 8
decoration time 45 minutes, plus drying

900 ml (1½ pint) pudding basin chocolate-
flavoured Medium Madeira Cake, made
with half the 4-egg mixture (see page 13)

25 x 20 cm (10 x 8 inch) oval cake board
or plate

cocktail sticks

1 large chocolate Muffin (see page 17), or a
large bought muffin, paper case removed

2 bought mini chocolate sponge rolls

2 bought sponge finger biscuits

single quantity Chocolate Fudge Icing (see
page 22)

100 g (3½ oz) pale blue ready-to-roll icing

sifted icing sugar, for dusting

2 foil-wrapped chocolate coins, unwrapped, or
2 jumbo chocolate buttons

15 g (½ oz) white ready-to-roll icing

2 blue mini candy-covered chocolate drops

1 brown candy-covered chocolate drop

pink paste food colouring

2 sugar flowers

50 cm (20 inch) fine ribbon (optional)

Tip

Make sure you remove the ribbon and
cocktail sticks before serving the cake to
birthday guests.

1 Level the basin cake top, if necessary. Put it, trimmed top downwards, on to the cake board or plate. Press 3 cocktail sticks into the domed top of the cake, then press the muffin on to the sticks so that the rounded top is facing forwards for the bear's head. Add the mini sponge rolls for the legs and sponge finger biscuits for the arms, attaching to the cake with more cocktail sticks.

2 Reserve 2 teaspoons of the fudge icing. Spread the remainder over the cake and rough up with the back of the knife so that it resembles fur. Leave for a few minutes to harden slightly.

3 Knead the blue icing on a surface lightly dusted with icing sugar until slightly softened. Roll out and cut out a waistcoat shape. Press on to the bear, adjusting the shape of the waistcoat, if necessary, with scissors.

4 Re-knead the trimmings. Roll small balls for the paws, flatten, then press on to the ends of the arms and legs. Add tiny flattened balls to the feet for claws.

5 To make the ears, press a small flattened ball of blue icing on to each chocolate coin or button, then press into the top of the head. Shape tiny flattened ovals of white icing for eyes and add mini candy-covered chocolate drops for eyeballs, sticking in place with dots of the reserved fudge icing. Add the brown candy-covered chocolate drop for the nose. Colour the remaining white icing pink, roll out and cut out a mouth shape. Press on to the bear's face. Add the sugar flowers for buttons, sticking in place with dots of fudge icing. Complete with a ribbon around the neck, if liked.

Mini duck ponds

makes 12
decoration time 30 minutes

12 Fairy Cakes (see page 16), or bought
  fairy cakes

single quantity Glacé Icing (see page 24)

blue paste food colouring

3 tablespoons desiccated coconut

green paste food colouring

300 g (10 oz) yellow ready-to-roll icing

sifted icing sugar, for dusting

25 g (1 oz) orange ready-to-roll icing

2 tablespoons Royal Icing (see page 25),
  coloured green, or 1 tube green
  writing icing

25 cm (10 inch) round cake board or plate

1 Level the cake tops, if necessary. Colour the glacé icing blue with the colouring, then spoon on to the cake tops and smooth with the back of the spoon.

2 Put the coconut in a small bowl with a little of the green colouring and mix with a spoon until pale green. Sprinkle around the edges of the blue icing 'ponds'.

3 Knead the yellow icing on a surface lightly dusted with icing sugar until slightly softened. Tear off small pieces and make 12 oval-shaped duck bodies 2.5 cm (1 inch) long and 12 small oval heads 2 cm (¾ inch) long. Press the heads on to the bodies and stick in place with a little water, if necessary.

4 Re-knead the trimmings, roll out and cut out six 5 cm (2 inch) rounds with a fluted biscuit cutter. Cut each round into quarters, then stick a pair of quarters on each duck as wings, with the fluted edge as the wing tips, using a little water.

5 Knead and roll out the orange icing. Shape tiny triangular beaks and stick on to the ducks with a little water. Sit the ducks on the mini ponds and use royal or writing icing to pipe on green eyes. Transfer to the cake board or plate.

Tip

As an alternative, Easter-themed, design, you could make smaller wings and transform the ducks into chickens, then sit them on nests of crumbled chocolate flake with mini chocolate eggs in the centre.

My first pony

serves 8–10
decoration time 45 minutes

1 Draw a horse's head on a piece of paper the same size as the cake. Cut it out and use as a template to cut the shape from the cake. Cut two triangular ears from the trimmings.

2 Cut the cake horizontally in half and sandwich back together with some of the butter icing. Spread the remaining butter icing thinly over the top and sides of the cake, adding the ears and covering them with butter icing. Transfer to the cake board or plate.

3 Knead the brown icing on a surface lightly dusted with icing sugar until slightly softened. Roll out the icing and use to cover the cake. Smooth in place with your fingertips dusted with icing sugar. Trim off the excess. Re-knead and wrap the trimmings. Mark a mouth with the handle of a small brush.

4 Knead and roll out the black icing. Cut strips for bridle and reins and place on the cake, sticking in position with a little water. Cut a circle of icing with an upturned piping nozzle then cut out a smaller circle with another piping tube. Position where the reins meet the bridle at the mouth.

5 Roll out a little of the brown trimmings, and cut out 2 brown ears and an eye socket. Press on to the cake, adding a black eyeball. Knead extra brown colouring into the remaining brown icing to darken. Re-roll the dark brown and black trimmings and cut petal shapes for the mane. Stick on to the neck with water. Add a red rosette (see page 74), if liked. Pipe your child's name or age on to the rosette, if liked.

30 x 23 x 5 cm (12 x 9 x 2 inch) roasting tin chocolate-flavoured Medium Madeira Cake (see page 13)

one-and-a-half quantity Butter Icing (see page 21)

38 x 33 cm (15 x 13 inch) oval cake board, covered with 500 g (1 lb) pale green ready-to-roll icing, or a plate

500 g (1 lb) brown ready-to-roll icing

sifted icing sugar, for dusting

150 g (5 oz) black ready-to-roll icing

brown paste food colouring

125 g (4 oz) red ready-to-roll icing (optional)

Tip

For a child who is regularly taking riding lessons, adapt the colouring to suit their favourite pony at the stables.

scary shark

serves 12
decoration time 1 hour

30 x 23 x 5 cm (12 x 9 x 2 inch) roasting tin
  Medium Madeira Cake (see page 13)

28 x 23 cm (11 x 9 inch) thin oval cake board

one-and-a-half quantity Butter Icing
  (see page 21), coloured red

500 g (1 lb) black ready-to-roll icing

sifted icing sugar, for dusting

125 g (4 oz) white ready-to-roll icing

2 yellow and black liquorice sweets

black paper

35 x 30 cm (14 x 12 inch) cake board or plate

Tip
Use black paste food colouring for a really
dark colour or buy ready-coloured black
icing from specialist cake-icing shops.

1 Put the cake on to a chopping board so the top is uppermost
and the short sides are facing you. Measure 12 cm (5 inches)
up from the bottom left-hand corner, repeat on the other side
and 19 cm (7½ inches) up in the centre then cut between the
marks in an arched line. Set aside for the shark's head. Cut a
10 cm (4 inch) deep semicircle from the remaining cake, using
the uncut edge as the base, for the jaw. Discard the trimmings.

2 Put the jaw on to the cake board with the curved edge almost
touching one end. Graduate the straight edge of the back of
the jaw so the other cake section will sit comfortably, then place
the shark's head on top, half on the jaw, half off, to make the
mouth. Fill in the gaps underneath the top cake with trimmings.

3 Spread the mouth area of the cakes thickly with butter icing,
then spread the rest thinly over the top and sides of the cake.

4 Knead and roll out one-third of the black icing to a long strip
and trim to 37.5 x 5 cm (15 x 2 inches). Carefully lift and
press around the jaw base and a little over the head base,
smoothing in place with your fingertips. Roll out the remaining
icing, curve one edge and press the curved edge up to the
curved edge on top of the shark's head. Drape over the
sides, down to the back of the cake board, and smooth in
place. Trim off the excess icing and reserve.

5 Cut triangles for teeth from the thinly rolled white icing. Press
the top teeth in place first, then the bottom teeth. Add 2
liquorice sweet eyeballs. Shape 2 black eyelids and press
over the eyeballs. Cut 3 fins 18 cm (7 inches) long and a tail
43 cm (17 inches) long from black paper. Fold along the
base of one fin and stand on the cake top. Put the other 2
fins and tail on the large cake board or plate, place the shark
cake on top then curl the end of the tail so that it stands up.

Timid tortoise

serves 8
decoration time 1 hour

1 Level the cake top, if necessary. Put, trimmed top downwards, on to a chopping board, cut horizontally in half and sandwich back together with some of the butter icing. Spread a little butter icing thinly all over the top and side of the cake then put it on to the cake board or plate.

2 Make a hexagon paper template by cutting a circle of paper 4 cm (1¾ inches) in diameter. (The top of a spice jar is an ideal size for this.) Fold in half then into three to make six segments. Cut a straight line from each tip of the fold to the other then open out.

3 Cut off one-quarter of the yellow icing, wrap and reserve. Knead the remaining yellow icing on a surface lightly dusted with icing sugar until slightly softened. Roll out thinly. Repeat with the pink and blue icing.

4 Cut out several hexagons. Put one yellow hexagon in the centre of the cake then arrange alternate-coloured shapes in 3 rings around the tortoise's shell, rolling and cutting the icing trimmings until the tortoise is completely covered.

5 Knead the remaining pink icing and shape four small legs and a head. Butt up against the cake. Knead and roll out the reserved yellow icing, shape into a long rope, then flatten with a rolling pin and trim to 62 cm (25 inches) long by 1 cm (½ inch) wide. Press around the base of the tortoise's shell. Shape the tortoise's eyes and eyelids from blue and pink icing and stick on to the cake with water. Make a mouth with a cocktail stick.

6 Decorate the cake board with sugar flowers, cut with different-sized plunger cutters (see page 32), if liked.

20 cm (8 inch) mixing bowl Small Madeira Cake (see page 12)

one-and-a-half quantity Butter Icing (see page 21)

28 cm (11 inch) thin round cake board, covered with 375 g (12 oz) pale green icing, or plate

375 g (12 oz) pale yellow ready-to-roll icing

sifted icing sugar, for dusting

375 g (12 oz) pale pink ready-to-roll icing

150 g (5 oz) pale blue ready-to-roll icing

few sugar flowers (optional)

Tip
You may find it easier to roll out small pieces of coloured icing with a child's rolling pin, making just enough hexagons for one ring at a time so that they don't dry out as you stick them on.

Fearless lion

serves 14–16
decoration time 30 minutes

23 cm (9 inch) deep round Large Madeira
    Cake (see page 13)

1 bought mini sponge roll

25 cm (10 inch) thin round cake board or plate

double quantity Butter Icing (see page 21)

yellow paste food colouring

red paste food colouring

black paste food colouring

200 g (7 oz) bar plain dark or milk chocolate

150 g (5 oz) white ready-to-roll icing

2 yellow and black liquorice sweets

Tips

- The butter icing could alternatively be
  coloured and flavoured with about 4
  teaspoons cocoa powder dissolved in
  1 tablespoon boiling water instead of
  using the food colouring, if preferred.
- If you are very short of time, use pieces
  of chocolate flake for the lion's mane
  and ready-coloured ready-to-roll icing.

1 Trim the top of the large round cake level, if needed. Put the cake on to a chopping board and lay the mini sponge roll on top in the centre for the lion's nose. Make 2 inverted 'V' cuts, each about 5 cm (2 inches) deep and 5 cm (2 inches) apart, beneath the nose to make the lion's jaw. Reserve the trimmings for the ears. Round the jaw with a small knife, then round the cheeks on either side.

2 Transfer the cake to the cake board or plate. Stick the ears in place with a little butter icing.

3 Reserve 1 teaspoon of the butter icing. Colour the remainder orange using a little each of the yellow and red colourings, then spread all over the top and side of the cake.

4 Turn the chocolate bar over so that the smooth side is uppermost. Run a swivel-bladed vegetable peeler over the smooth side to make curls (see page 32). Press the chocolate curls around the top edge of the cake for the lion's mane using the flat edge of a round-bladed knife.

5 Knead and roll 2 small balls of white icing, flatten and shape into thin ovals, then press on to the face for eyes. Add the sweets for eyeballs, sticking them in place with a little of the reserved butter icing.

6 Colour two-thirds of the remaining white icing deep orange, shape into a curled tongue and press in place. Colour the remaining icing black, shape into 2 flat rounds, then press on to the base of the nose. Add small indentations with the end of a cocktail stick. Store in a cool place until ready to serve.

Dancing dolphins

serves 10
decoration time 1 hour

Large round Quick-mix Sandwich Cake
  (see page 14)

double quantity Butter Icing (see page 21)

25 cm (10 inch) round cake board or plate

375 g (12 oz) white ready-to-roll icing

sifted icing sugar, for dusting

ice blue paste food colouring

250 g (8 oz) dark blue ready-to-roll icing

1 metre (39 inches) x 4 cm (1½ inch) wide blue
  chiffon ribbon

1 Sandwich the cakes together with a little butter icing, then spread butter icing thinly around the side. Put on to the cake board or plate.

2 Knead the white icing on a surface lightly dusted with icing sugar until slightly softened. Knead in a little blue colouring until a pale even blue, then mix in a little more colouring until marbled with blue streaks.

3 Shape the icing into a long rope, then flatten with a rolling pin and trim to a strip 65 x 10 cm (26 x 4 inches). Press around the side of the cake, pressing the extra width over the top edge of the cake. Trim off any excess from the join.

4 Partially mix a little blue colouring into the remaining butter icing until it becomes marbled. Reserve 1 tablespoon of the icing, then swirl the remainder over the top of the cake to resemble the sea.

5 Knead the dark blue icing until softened slightly. Shape into 2 dolphins about 12.5 cm (5 inches) long by making a thick sausage shape and squeezing a nose at one end and a tapering tail at the other. Next, shape a dolphin head about 6 cm (2½ inches) long. Shape the remaining icing into small fins. Stick on to the dolphins with a little water or dots of butter icing. Make eyes by pressing a cocktail stick into the icing.

6 Arrange the dolphins on the cake, propping them up on pieces of pale blue icing so they look as if they are jumping. Spread the reserved butter icing around the icing support to resemble lapping waves. Tie the ribbon in a pretty bow around the cake.

Tip

Instead of dolphins, why not try modelling a boat with a fisherman or a sailor onboard out of ready-to-roll icing?

Seasonal treats

Valentine cup cakes

makes 12
decoration time 30 minutes

single quantity Butter Icing (see page 21)

pink paste food colouring

12 Fairy Cakes (see page 16) or bought fairy
    cakes, with silver foil paper cases

200 g (7 oz) red ready-to-roll icing

sifted icing sugar, for dusting

10 chocolate sticks

75 g (3 oz) pale pink ready-to-roll icing

large round or square plate

1 Colour the butter icing pale pink with a little of the colouring. Level the tops of the cakes, if needed. Spread the tops of the cakes with an equal quantity of the butter icing.

2 Knead the red icing on a surface lightly dusted with icing sugar until slightly softened. Roll out and cut out twelve 5 cm (2 inch) hearts with a biscuit cutter, re-kneading and rolling out the trimmings as necessary.

3 Press the heart shapes on to 10 of the cakes. Cut the remaining 2 hearts in half with a zigzag line to symbolize a broken heart. Separate the halves slightly, then press on to the 2 remaining cakes.

4 For Cupid's arrows, break each chocolate stick in half, press one half into the centre of each unbroken heart and the other half as if coming out of the edge of the cake. Knead and roll out the pink ready-to-roll icing, cut out triangular arrow tips and 'V'-shaped feathers and stick on to the chocolate sticks with a little water or with tiny dots of butter icing from the scrapings in the bowl. Arrange on the plate and sprinkle the plate with heart-shaped foil graffiti, if liked.

Tip

Instead of adding the Cupid's arrows, pipe on boys' and girls' names with tubes of coloured writing icing.

Easter bunnies

makes 12
decoration time 30 minutes

12 Fairy Cakes (see page 16) or bought
   fairy cakes

single quantity Butter Icing (see page 21)

12 large white marshmallows

4 large pink marshmallows

12 mini white marshmallows

24 blue mini candy-covered chocolate drops

12 small square pink sweets

2 tablespoons Royal Icing (see page 25),
   coloured red, or 1 tube red fine
   writing icing

25 g (1 oz) pale pink ready-to-roll icing

sifted icing sugar, for dusting

large round or square plate

1 Level the tops of the cakes, if needed. Spread the tops of the
   cakes with an equal amount of the butter icing.

2 Cut the large white marshmallows in half. With the cut side
   uppermost, squeeze the corners to form into ear shapes.
   Press 2 on to each cake, cut side uppermost. Cut the pink
   marshmallows in half, then each half into slices. Press a slice
   on top of each ear.

3 Cut the mini white marshmallows in half and press the cut
   sides downwards on to the rabbit faces for cheeks. Add blue
   candy-covered chocolate drops for eyes and square pink
   sweets for noses. Pipe a mouth on to each rabbit with red
   royal or writing icing.

4 Knead the pale pink icing on a surface lightly dusted with
   icing sugar until slightly softened. Roll out and cut tiny strips
   for whiskers. Press on to the rabbits. Arrange on a plate and
   store in a cool place until ready to serve.

Tip

To save time on a party day, the cakes
may be made in advance, spread with the
butter icing and then frozen. Add the facial
features once the cakes have defrosted.

Ghostly ghoul

serves 10
decoration time 30 minutes

1 Put the cake on to a chopping board and cut into a long oval face shape. Curve the sides slightly to indicate hollow cheeks and a jaw. Cut the cake horizontally in half and sandwich back together with some of the butter icing. Spread the remaining butter icing thinly over the top and sides of the cake.

2 Cut off 200 g (7 oz) of the white icing, wrap the remainder and reserve. Knead on a surface lightly dusted with icing sugar until slightly softened. Add a little black colouring and knead until partially mixed and marbled. Roll out the icing thinly, drape over the cake board and smooth with your fingertips dusted with icing sugar. Trim off the excess.

3 Lift the cake on to the board. Pull off small pieces of the reserved white icing and shape into sausage shapes. Press on to the cake for eyebrows, lips, nose and frown lines. Roll out the remaining white icing and drape over the cake to cover completely, smoothing over the raised areas with your fingertips dusted with icing sugar. Trim off the excess.

4 Colour the trimmings black. Roll out a small ball of icing and cut a heart-shaped nose. Divide the remaining icing into thirds and shape each third into a small sausage. Flatten and shape into eyes and a mouth. Press on to the cake, sticking in place with a little water.

30 x 23 x 5 cm (12 x 9 x 2 inch) roasting tin
Medium Madeira Cake (see page 13)

double quantity Butter Icing (see page 21)

625 g (1¼ lb) white ready-to-roll icing

sifted icing sugar, for dusting

black paste food colouring

30 x 25 cm (12 x 10 inch) oval cake board

Tip

You may find it easier to dust the cake board with a little icing sugar and roll the marbled icing straight on to the board with a rolling pin.

spooky spiders

makes 12
decoration time 1 hour

12 Fairy Cakes (see page 16) or bought
  fairy cakes, with silver foil paper cases

single quantity Butter Icing (see page 21)

500 g (1 lb) purple ready-to-roll icing

sifted icing sugar, for dusting

18 black liquorice Catherine wheels

12 chocolate-covered marshmallow teacakes

24 pink candy-covered chocolate drops

24 mini blue candy-covered chocolate drops

1 tube black writing icing

large round or square plate

125 g (4 oz) pink or dark blue ready-to-roll
  icing

1 Level the tops of the cakes, if needed. Spread the top of each cake with a little butter icing. Knead the purple icing on a surface lightly dusted with icing sugar until slightly softened. Roll out and stamp out twelve 6 cm (2½ inch) rounds with a plain biscuit cutter. Press one on top of each cake. Re-knead and roll out the trimmings. Stamp out twelve 3.5 cm (1½ inch) plain rounds and press one on to each cake for a head.

2 Add a little butter icing to the centre of each cake. Unroll the liquorice and cut into 10 cm (4 inch) lengths. Add to each cake for legs. Cover the ends on each body with a teacake.

3 Stick 2 of the larger pink candy-covered chocolate drops on to each head for eyes with a little butter icing. Add the mini blue candy-covered chocolate drops for eyeballs and pipe black vertical lines down the centre with writing icing and tiny V-shaped nostrils.

4 Transfer the spiders to a plate and add small balls of pink or blue icing to the ends of the liquorice legs for feet.

Tip

For children who do not like liquorice, snip coloured jelly strips, such as those used for the grid in the Noughts and Crosses cake on page 60, into legs instead.

Jack-o-lantern

serves 8
decoration time 30 minutes

20 cm (8 inch) mixing bowl Small Madeira Cake (see page 12)

double quantity Butter Icing (see page 21)

yellow and red or orange paste food colourings

23 cm (9 inch) thin round cake board or large plate

50 g (2 oz) black ready-to-roll icing

sifted icing sugar, for dusting

125 g (4 oz) green ready-to-roll icing

1 Colour the butter icing orange with a little each of the yellow and red or orange colourings. Cut the cake horizontally in half and sandwich back together with some of the butter icing. Transfer the cake to the cake board or plate.

2 Spread a little butter icing thinly all over the cake to stick the crumbs in place, then spread thickly with more butter icing and smooth in downward lines with the back of a knife.

3 Knead the black icing on a surface lightly dusted with icing sugar until slightly softened. Roll out and cut out a large smiling mouth. Cut out small squares or triangles for missing teeth. Press on to the cake. Cut out triangles for eyes and a nose and press in place on the cake.

4 Knead and roll out the green icing. Cut out leaves of different sizes, mark on veins with a small knife then arrange on the cake top, curling and folding them slightly. Re-knead and roll out the trimmings. Cut long thin strips and curl these in and around the leaves to resemble tendrils.

Tip

Add the colouring little by little; you will find that you need less paste colouring than when colouring ready-to-roll icing.

Playful polar bears

serves 20
decoration time 1 hour, plus drying

23 cm (9 inch) deep round Large Madeira
  Cake (see page 13)

one-and-a-half quantity Butter Icing
  (see page 21)

28 cm (11 inch) thin round cake board or plate

750 g (1½ lb) pale blue ready-to-roll icing

sifted icing sugar, for dusting

single quantity Royal Icing (see page 25)

3 tablespoons desiccated coconut

250 g (8 oz) white ready-to-roll icing

black writing icing or an edible black icing pen

Tip

This cake could also be made into a
teddy's tea party by covering the cake in
pale green ready-to-roll icing, colouring
the royal icing pink and spreading it into
a smaller table-cloth shape. Add yellow
bears and a dolls' house tea service with
tiny plates and cups.

1 Trim the top of the cake level, if needed. Cut the cake
horizontally in half and sandwich back together with butter
icing. Put it on the cake board or plate and spread the
remaining butter icing over the top and side of the cake.

2 Knead the blue icing on a surface lightly dusted with icing
sugar until slightly softened. Roll out and use to cover the top
and side of the cake. Smooth in place with your fingertips
dusted with icing sugar. Trim off the excess.

3 Spoon the royal icing over the top of the cake and spread it
so that it dribbles over the sides. Ease into icicle-like shapes
with the point of a knife. Spread a little icing in patches on
the board or plate and up the side of the cake. Sprinkle with
the coconut, letting some fall on to the cake board or plate.

4 Knead the white ready-to-roll icing until slightly softened.
Shape 5 different-sized ovals of icing for the polar bear
bodies. Shape 5 round heads and make a small pinch in
each for a muzzle. Press the heads on to the bodies. Arrange
on the cake, sitting, lying or stretching up the side of the
cake. For the standing bear, you may need to attach the
body to the side of the cake with some royal icing scrapings
from the bowl. Shape sausage-like arms and legs, making
them slightly thicker where they join on to the body. To make
the ears, roll tiny balls of icing, then flatten and press on to
the heads, sticking in place with a little water. Roll any
remaining trimmings into snowballs of various sizes.

5 Leave the bears to harden, then pipe or write on face details
with black writing icing or an icing pen.

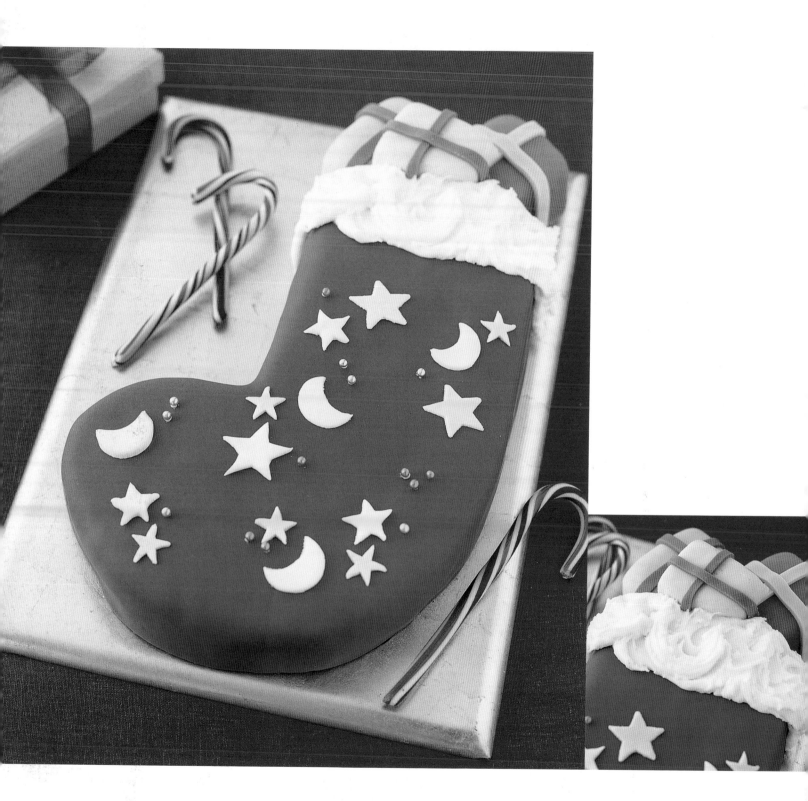

Christmas stocking

serves 10
decoration time 1 hour

1 Put the cake on to a chopping board and cut into a stocking shape about 11 cm (4½ inches) wide at the top of the leg. Cut 3 different-sized gifts from the trimmings and set aside. Cut the cake horizontally in half and sandwich back together with some butter icing. Spread a little butter icing very thinly over the top and sides of the cake and over the gifts. Transfer the stocking cake to the cake board or plate.

2 Knead the deep blue icing on a surface lightly dusted with icing sugar until slightly softened. Roll out and drape over the whole of the cake and smooth in place with your fingertips dusted with icing sugar. Trim off the excess.

3 Spread most of the royal icing over the top of the stocking and down both sides, then rough it up so that it resembles fleecy lining. Spoon the remaining icing into a greaseproof paper piping bag and snip off the tip (see page 31).

4 Knead and roll out the white icing and cut out rounds using a small round biscuit cutter, then cut partway into the rounds to make crescent moons. Cut star shapes with different-sized cutters. Stick the shapes on to the stocking with piped dots of royal icing. Repeat with a little pale pink icing. Add extra dots of piped icing and stick on rainbow pearls or silver balls.

5 Knead and roll out the deep pink, pale blue and remaining pale pink icings and cover one gift in each colour. Cut ribbons from the trimmings and stick on to the gifts with royal icing. Position at the top of the stocking. Add the candy canes to the cake board or plate.

30 x 23 x 5 cm (12 x 9 x 2 inch) roasting tin Medium Madeira Cake (see page 13)

double quantity Butter Icing (see page 21)

36 x 25 cm (14 x 10 inch) rectangular cake board or plate

375 g (12 oz) deep blue ready-to-roll icing

sifted icing sugar, for dusting

half quantity Royal Icing (see page 25)

75 g (3 oz) white ready-to-roll icing

75 g (3 oz) pale pink ready-to-roll icing

few rainbow pearls or edible silver balls

65 g (2½ oz) deep pink ready-to-roll icing

50 g (2 oz) pale blue ready-to-roll icing

selection of candy canes

Tip

If using a cake board, you may like to cover it with pale pink ready-to-roll icing before adding the cake.

Smiling snowman

serves 12
decoration time 1 hour

2 x 900 ml (1½ pint) pudding basin Medium
    Madeira Cakes (see page 13)

single quantity vanilla-flavoured Butter Icing
    (see page 21)

2 tablespoons apricot jam

15 cm (6 inch) thin round cake board or plate

1 Muffin (see page 17) or bought large muffin,
    paper case removed

triple quantity Royal icing (see page 25)

15 g (½ oz) black ready-to-roll icing

sifted icing sugar, for dusting

25 g (1 oz) orange ready-to-roll icing

50 g (2 oz) red ready-to-roll icing

25 g (1 oz) yellow ready-to-roll icing

Tip

The snowman can alternatively be
sandwiched together and covered with a
double quantity of vanilla or lemon butter
icing (see page 21) instead of royal icing.

1 Level the basin cake tops, if necessary, and sandwich the trimmed tops together with the butter icing to make the snowman's body. Spread jam thinly all over the outside of the cakes to stick the crumbs in place. Stand the cake upright on the cake board or plate. Press the muffin on to the body so that the domed part of the muffin forms the snowman's face. Spread the muffin with the remaining jam.

2 Spoon the royal icing over the cakes to cover completely, spreading it as you go with a round-bladed knife and pulling it into peaks with the back of the knife. Be careful not to smear the jam into the icing.

3 Knead the black icing on a surface lightly dusted with icing sugar until slightly softened and shape black eyes and 'coal' buttons. Press on to the snowman. Knead the orange icing and shape a tiny piece for the snowman's 'carrot' nose. Press on to the snowman's face.

4 Knead the red icing, shape a tiny rope mouth and add to the face. Shape half the remaining red icing into a round and press on to the snowman's head for a hat.

5 Knead the yellow icing and shape into a rope 18 cm (7 inches) long. Repeat with the remaining orange and red icing. Twist the 3 colours together, then roll out to flatten. Trim to a 36 x 2.5 cm (14 x 1 inch) strip. Make small cuts in either end for a fringe, then wrap around the snowman as a scarf. Re-knead and roll out the trimmings, fringe one side, then roll up and add to the top of the hat for a bobble.

Index

Acknowledgements

Executive Editor Nicola Hill
Editor Leanne Bryan
Executive Art Editor Karen Sawyer
Designer Lisa Tai
Photographer Lis Parsons
Home Economist Sara Lewis
Props Stylist Rachel Jukes
Senior Production Controller
  Martin Croshaw
Picture Librarian Sopie Delpech

Picture Acknowledgements

Special Photography:
©Octopus Publishing Group Limited/
Lis Parsons

Other Photography:
Octopus Publishing Group Limited/
Gareth Sambidge 16 bottom

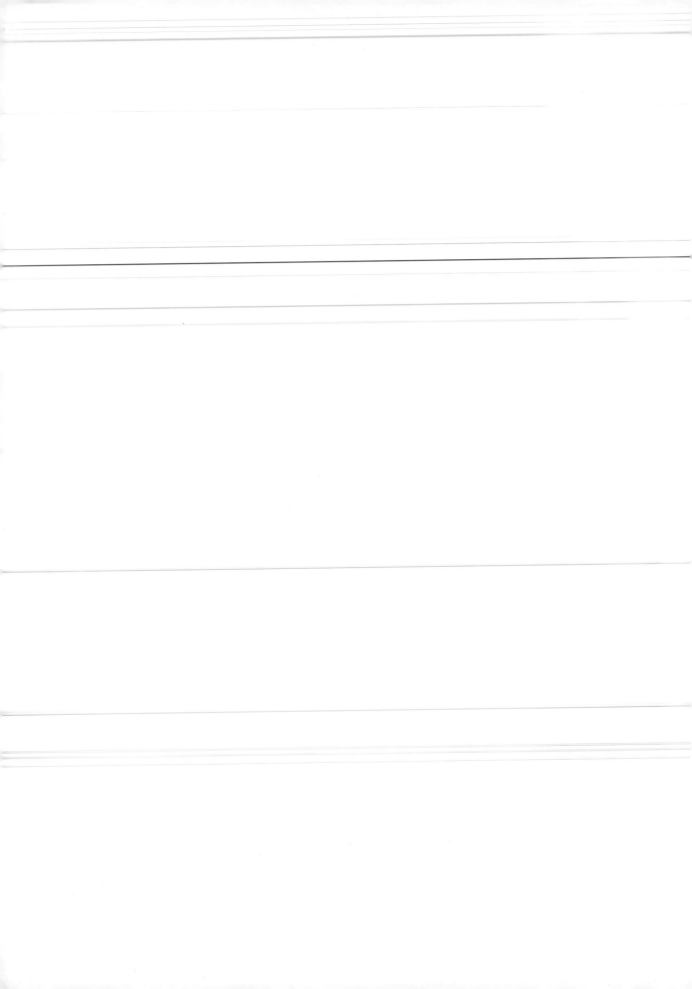